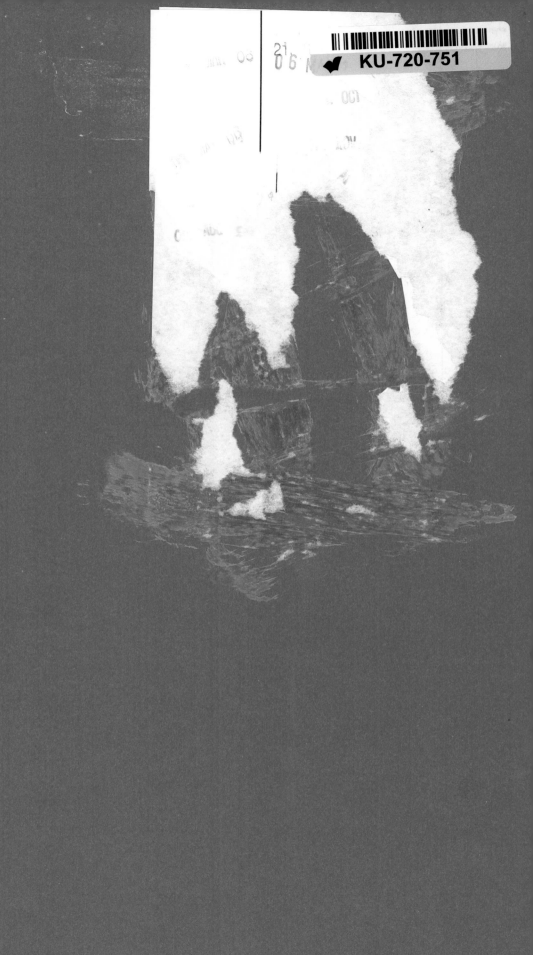

DISCOVER
PAPIER MÂCHÉ

DISCOVER
PAPIER MÂCHÉ

40 ORIGINAL PROJECTS TO BUILD YOUR MODELLING SKILLS

LIZ MANSON

HAMLYN

566441

First published in Great Britain in 1995 by Hamlyn
an imprint of Reed Consumer Books Limited,
Michelin House, 81 Fulham Road, London SW3 6RB
and Auckland, Melbourne, Singapore and Toronto

TEXT AND PHOTOGRAPHS © 1995
REED INTERNATIONAL BOOKS LIMITED

SERIES PROJECT MANAGER: **MARY LAMBERT**
SERIES PROJECT ART EDITOR: **PRUE BUCKNALL**
ART EDITOR: **ALISON SHACKLETON**
EXECUTIVE EDITOR: **JUDITH MORE**
ART DIRECTOR: **JACQUI SMALL**

PHOTOGRAPHS BY: **LUCY MASON**

The publishers have made every effort to ensure that all instructions
given in this book are accurate and safe, but they cannot accept liability
for any resulting injury, damage or loss to either person or property
whether direct or consequential and howsoever arising. The author and
publishers will be grateful for any information which will assist them in
keeping future editions up to date.

ISBN: 0 600 585921

DTP ALISON SHACKLETON
ORIGINATION BY MANDARIN, SINGAPORE
PRINTED IN HONG KONG

CONTENTS

INTRODUCTION

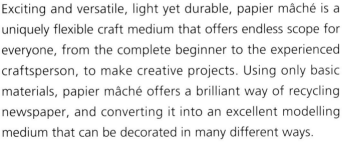

Exciting and versatile, light yet durable, papier mâché is a uniquely flexible craft medium that offers endless scope for everyone, from the complete beginner to the experienced craftsperson, to make creative projects. Using only basic materials, papier mâché offers a brilliant way of recycling newspaper, and converting it into an excellent modelling medium that can be decorated in many different ways.

There has been a huge growth in interest in papier mâché in the last few years. This seems to have begun partly as a reaction from artists and craftspeople to the more uniform objects we are surrounded by in our modern technology-led world. The nature of papier mâché is such that no one object ever looks the same as another. And while it is possible with certain techniques to achieve a highly finished, smooth effect, most people value the quirky irregularities and roughness of the traditional finish.

It is no coincidence that contemporary papier mâché has been strongly influenced by primitive art and modern ethnic designs from Africa and Latin America, as these are both characterized by vibrant decoration and a simple, direct approach to modelling and construction. There has also been a great interest in surface finishes, particularly those that simulate the ageing process of burnished metals and weathered stone.

Papercraft originated in Ancient Egypt with papyrus, which was made from the pulped stems of water reeds. Paper made from a rag and net pulp was invented in China in the 1st century AD. Centuries on, it was the import of fashionable lacquered wooden cabinets from China in the late 17th century that led to a rapid growth of papier mâché production in Europe, as the Europeans sought to imitate the Oriental lacquer techniques. The intense heat needed to bake the lacquer cabinets tended to warp the wood, but the European furniture makers then discovered the process of papier mâché, which was heat resistant.

Oddly enough it was an English printer John Baskerville, who together with his apprentice Henry Clay, perfected the technique of pasting panels of paper together in 1772.

Meanwhile, many amateurs were discovering the pulp method, japan ware and lacquer techniques.

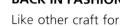

BACK IN FASHION

Like other craft forms, papier mâché has passed in and out of fashion over the centuries. Today, it is not only once again in vogue, but also successfully established as a major craft form. Craft exhibitions, shops and markets now sell a huge range of brightly coloured papier mâché ware that is produced all over the world.

Newsprint is still the main paper source to make papier mâché, but other types of papers, such as brown wrapping or cartridge paper, can be used to vary the texture and strength of objects. All the projects in this book are made from two simple methods: the layered, where torn strips of newspaper are built up to form the shape of the object; and the pulped, where newspaper is soaked and pulped to create a good modelling material. A dried pulp product that only needs water to be added can be bought from craft stores if you have limited time, but it is so easy to make your own pulp and it keeps in the refrigerator, so you don't have to use it all straightaway (*see Materials and Techniques pp. 8–15*). By following the simple step-by-step instructions in the techniques section you really can get to know the papier mâché medium.

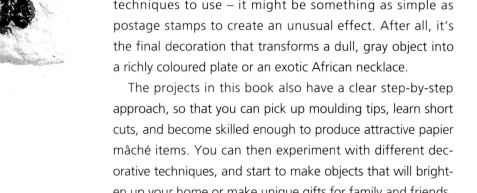

THE FINAL PRODUCT

When you decorate your papier mâché objects you will want to experiment with finishes and effects. In this book there is detailed guidance on what painting and decorative techniques to use – it might be something as simple as postage stamps to create an unusual effect. After all, it's the final decoration that transforms a dull, gray object into a richly coloured plate or an exotic African necklace.

The projects in this book also have a clear step-by-step approach, so that you can pick up moulding tips, learn short cuts, and become skilled enough to produce attractive papier mâché items. You can then experiment with different decorative techniques, and start to make objects that will brighten up your home or make unique gifts for family and friends.

MATERIALS AND TECHNIQUES

All the projects in this book use the two basic papier mâché methods: layered or pulped. Before starting any of the projects it is advisable to read through all the instructions and study the pictures for the whole project. Check that you have all the materials and equipment you will need, particularly the basic ingredients that are outlined here.

EQUIPMENT

Much of the basic equipment needed to make papier mâché is readily available in most homes. Check that craft knives are sharp before you start cutting card or trimming papier mâché, and ensure that any paintbrushes being used are in good order and won't drop hairs in the varnish. It is best to work on a large, clear flat surface – an offcut from a laminated kitchen surface or an old baking board is an ideal choice.

YOU WILL NEED
For the layered method
- Bucket for the newspaper strips
- Cotton buds for bead moulds and applying releasing agent
- Paintbrushes to apply PVA medium to the strips of newspaper. A flat, square-ended type of paintbrush is best
- Hair dryer to speed up the overall drying process
- Craft knife for cutting card
- Scissors

For the pulped method
- Bowl or bucket for soaking the newspaper
- Saucepan to boil the newspaper in
- Sieve
- Cotton buds for bead moulds and applying releasing agent
- Wooden spoon
- Hand-held blender or whisk to pulp papier mâché
- A roller, rolling pin or large bottle to roll out the pulp
- Craft knife
- Clingfilm to hold still-wet projects – they can be left to dry on this
- Baking foil to cover unused pulp and prevent it drying out
- Hair dryer for speeding up the overall drying process

MAKING PAPIER MÂCHÉ

Both the methods described here give particularly good results, producing an easily workable papier mâché. The layered method, as it name suggests, is done by building up layer upon layer of newspaper strips; the pulped method is a good medium for modelling and sculpting.

Simple household equipment is needed for the layered method (below), while the pulped method (bottom) requires a few more accessories, such as a blender and also a saucepan.

THE LAYERED METHOD

THE INGREDIENTS

- Double sheets of newspaper – torn into strips or squares, according to the type of project to be made
- PVA medium – widely available in craft stores, this makes an excellent glue and easily washes off hands
- Water – to thin the PVA medium a little, and to help saturate the newspaper

- Releasing agent – you will need an oil-based releasing agent – petroleum jelly is ideal – to help remove the dried papier mâché from its mould. Without this it is almost impossible to remove the papier mâché intact
- Brown paper tape – gummed brown paper tape is very useful to join cardboard and papier mâché together. It is very strong, and can safely be pulped on, or layered over

1

2

1 Tear strips along the grain of the newspaper. These should generally be about 1in (2.5cm) in width. Some projects, however, require smaller squares to go around awkward shapes, while others, such as the tea tray project (*see pp. 84–85*), need broader 2in (5cm) strips that work better when forming a large, flat surface.

2 Thin the PVA medium with a little water and apply to the strips with the pasting brush. Alternatively, you can soak the strips in the solution.

THE PULPED METHOD

THE INGREDIENTS

(Makes enough pulp for each project unless otherwise detailed)

- Double sheets of newspaper – torn into pieces ready to be soaked.
- Water – to soak and boil the newspaper
- PVA medium – the glue used to hold the pulp together
- Linseed oil – makes the pulp supple and easy to handle
- Oil of cloves – has natural fungicidal properties and prevents mould from forming on papier mâché. It is widely available from chemists
- Releasing agent – petroleum jelly is ideal to use, but other oil-based substances, such as liquid detergent, can also be used to prevent the pulp from sticking fast in its mould
- Brown paper tape – used to tape card together when forming moulds

THE PULPED METHOD

1 Take the double sheets of newspaper and tear into pieces no larger than 1in (2.5cm) square. Soak in water for at least 8 hours, ideally 24 hours.

2 Drain the paper and boil in a pan of water on the hob for about 25 minutes to loosen the newspaper fibres.

3 Remove the saucepan from the heat, cool, and pour the contents into a sieve, shaking out any excess water.

4 Tip the paper into a bowl, and use a hand-held blender or whisk to reduce the paper to a pulp. The alternative method is to use a pestle and mortar.

5 Add in 3 tablespoons of PVA medium, 1 tablespoon of linseed oil and 3 drops of oil of cloves to the pulp and mix thoroughly with a wooden spoon.

6 The pulp can now be shaped into solid lumps, ready for use. It can also be wrapped in baking foil and stored in a refrigerator (for up to a month) until needed.

PULP TIPS

● Use a broadsheet, rather than tabloid, newspaper as the type of fibres in the newsprint make a stronger product.

● Wallpaper paste can be used instead of PVA medium, although it may contain a chemical fungicide, so you should avoid any direct contact with it.

1

2

3

4

5

6

CHOOSING A MOULD

When deciding on a mould that is suitable for your papier mâché project, one of the main priorities is to make sure that you will be able to release the project cleanly from the mould without causing any tearing or breakage.

For example, when choosing a bowl or dish, avoid one where the main opening is smaller than the bulk of the object, which would make it impossible to release the papier mâché. However, the more experienced craftsperson might feel confident enough to remove the papier mâché by cutting away sections using a craft knife, then refixing them with glue and brown tape and reinforcing the joins with layers of papier mâché. This is a tricky process and is not recommended for a beginner to attempt.

The chances are that you have many plates and bowls around your home that would make suitable moulds, but do remember they could be out of action for up to several weeks as the pulp or layers are added and left to dry. A good alternative source would be a jumble sale or boot sale where all manner of tableware turns up at virtually giveaway prices. It doesn't matter if the mould is made from china, metal or plastic as long as it is the right shape.

Kitchenware and tableware that are suitable for use as moulds include:

● Shallow salad dish – broad with a wide opening
● Soap dish
● Cereal bowl
● Various plates
● Baking sheet
● Spoons

Many different objects, including natural ones, make interesting moulds, as do many other items of household and garden bric-a-brac, including:
● Leaves
● Shells
● Avocado stones
● Balloons – ideal for making masks
● Cardboard tubes
● String
● Wire
● Modelling clay
● Cotton buds – pulp "beads" can be neatly formed on them

WIRE SUPPORTS

Larger projects may be made using the layered method of papier mâché over chicken wire, which is a strong but malleable support. Copper wire and fuse wire are ideal to create simple shapes or maquettes. You can mould pulp straight onto these when the wires are "knitted" together (see p. 46).

MODELLING CLAY

You can use modelling clay for building shapes on which to apply papier mâché, or you can make the necessary mould and fill it with pulp.

USING PAPIER MÂCHÉ ON A MOULD

Before you start to layer or pulp your papier mâché onto your chosen mould, check that you have all the necessary equipment and ingredients to hand, and that the mould you are using is clean and thoroughly dry. Work on a clear, clean surface and try to avoid creating any unnecessary clutter.

Always be on the lookout for potential moulds for papier mâché, for example,

items that normally get thrown away, such as yogurt cartons, shampoo bottles and plastic lids, are all suitable.

If you are using modelling clay as your mould to work on, you can leave it to harden in the refrigerator before applying the releasing agent, as it becomes very soft with continual handling.

When you are making wire structures for pulping or layering onto, have some wire cutters to hand, as normal scissors will just blunt in seconds if you attempt to cut wire with them.

LAYERING PAPIER MÂCHÉ ONTO A MOULD

MATERIALS
1 large dinner plate
Petroleum jelly
PVA medium, thinned half and half with water in a bowl
Flat-ended pasting brush
Newspaper, torn into 1in (2.5cm) strips in a bucket
Kitchen paper
Scissors

1 Prepare the dinner plate by smearing petroleum jelly (the releasing agent) over the entire surface that will be covered with papier mâché strips, and also onto the rim of the plate.

2 Brush the thinned PVA glue onto the torn strips of newspaper. Lay them horizontally across the mould overlapping each strip slightly. When you have completed this first layer, set aside to dry for several hours. Each layer must be absolutely hard and dry before you apply the next.

3 For the next layer of papier mâché work in exactly the same way, but apply the strips vertically on the plate. This will help to make a stronger and smoother papier mâché. It doesn't matter if the strips extend beyond the edge of the mould, but make sure that the whole of the mould is covered by each layer.

4 When you have built up eight layers of papier mâché and they are all hard and dry, gently release the project from the mould. Remove any residue of petroleum jelly with the kitchen paper, and then trim with scissors around the edge of the papier mâché mould to make an even and neat shape.

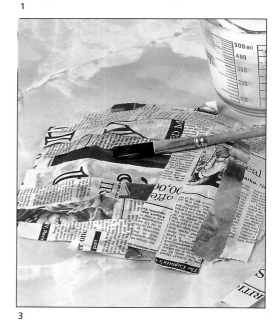

1

2

3

4

PULPING PAPIER MÂCHÉ ONTO A MOULD

MATERIALS
1 large dinner plate

Petroleum jelly

Papier mâché pulp
(see pp. 9–10)

Kitchen paper

Scissors or craft knife

1 Take the large dinner plate and cover the entire surface that will be coated with papier mâché pulp with petroleum jelly to act as a releasing agent.

2 Take a quantity of pulped papier mâché and apply a layer about ¼in (6mm) thick over the surface of the upturned plate. Papier mâché pulp has a tendency to shrink in the drying process, and it may be necessary to apply an additional layer to the first layer, while still damp, to increase the thickness. Leave the pulp to dry for about a week, or until it feels hard and dry.

3 When the papier mâché is fully dry, and you are happy that you have the right thickness of pulp, gently ease the shape from the mould. Remove any traces of petroleum jelly with kitchen paper and trim any uneven edges with scissors or a craft knife.

1

2

3

TIPS

● The drying process for both pulp and layered papier mâché projects can be accelerated by the use of a hair dryer for about ten minutes at a time.

● Papier mâché moulded on card can be dried and hardened in a microwave oven for up to one minute, but keep a close eye on this process and do not leave the oven unattended.

● The residue from the releasing agent can be removed with a spirit such as lighter fuel, but take great care when using this as it is inflammable and always keep away from children.

● A butter knife may help remove papier mâché that appears to be stuck fast to a mould. Gently ease the knife around the mould and the papier mâché, but avoid using any great force as this might damage both the mould and the papier mâché.

CARDBOARD
Cardboard comes in various thicknesses and is ideal for papier mâché bases and moulds. Boxes can be obtained from supermarkets.

13

You can use many different items other than paints, such as stamps and shells, to decorate your finished papier mâché objects. Ribbons, screw eyes and jewellery fittings can also be bought to finish other papier mâché projects.

DECORATING AND FINISHING

Once papier mâché objects have reached the gray and hardened stage, they simply need some added colour or lacquer finish to bring them to life. After you have trimmed away any excess material from the object, you may want to smooth down the rough edges with a nail file. Pulped papier mâché can look good with a mildly ragged texture. But if this look does not appeal to you, it is possible to smooth over the surface with some wood filler to produce a more even and consistent finish.

USING AN UNDERCOAT
Before you can apply any decoration or paint to the dried papier mâché, it needs to be given an undercoat. Fast-drying

Apply acrylic gesso onto hardened papier mâché with a paintbrush. Check that any traces of releasing agent have been removed, and that any irregularities have been trimmed as necessary.

acrylic gesso is perfect for this job as it gives a thick, extremely smooth layer of paint that provides an ideal surface to take a wide range of paint and ink finishes. Household emulsion is less expensive to use, but is more liable to crack. If you do use it, a matte vinyl finish will give a satisfactory undercoat if it is carefully applied in at least two layers.

PAINTING TECHNIQUES
Each project in this book gives a separate and detailed description on how to apply both paint and decoration, so that you can produce a papier mâché object that is very close to the illustrated project. You may feel confident right from the start to experiment with different types of paints and colours to create your own designs and special effects – the choice is entirely yours. But for the first few projects it is best to follow the guidance given.

You can also use a sponge to dab on the paint and create different, subtle and mottled effects. Make a stencil out of stiff card and then dab a design directly onto your project. By rubbing away some of the paint you can produce a translucent effect.

You can also build up thin coats of inks to produce rich, overlapping colours with a lacquer effect. Try blending colours on top of each other and produce a "distressed" effect by rubbing the surface with an abrasive cloth, revealing the other colours beneath. The possibilities at the painting stage are endless, so enjoy experimenting and be bold with your techniques.

DECORATING TOOLS
● Paintbrushes – it's worth investing in a few good-quality brushes before you start decorating. Use a fine brush for detail, and a larger one for areas of flat colour
● Acrylic gesso – to use as an undercoat
● Emulsion paint – ideally a matte vinyl finish to use as an alternative to acrylic gesso
● Drawing inks – these should really be a trade secret as they give such wonderful rich, translucent colours. Inks also mix well with poster and acrylic paints. You can achieve superb effects by building up layers of colours
● Metallic pens and metallic and pearlized

acrylic paints – these are are really good for achieving special effects
● Acrylic paints – offer very good coverage and strong colours
● Poster paints – useful in their own right and effective as a base for paint or ink
● Tissue paper – this can create interesting and delicate textures and subtle colours when glued down in overlapping layers or brushed with inks
● Foil paper – an interesting paper to give bold, rich highlights. It is especially dramatic when used against a solid, dark background, such as black.

Also look out for potential decoration in the form of attractive wrappings and sweet papers. Bus tickets, stamps and other printed items can provide visual interest when used creatively and are well worth saving.

YOU MAY ALSO NEED
● Ribbons – to thread on masks and plaques
● Shells – to press into a papier mâché pulp to make ornate, whimsical decoration
● Beads, earring findings and jewellery stems – useful items for making earrings
● Pliers – a small pair is ideal for making jewellery items
● Wire
● Strong glue
● Screw eyes – from DIY stores, these are used to hang finished projects

VARNISHING
Varnishing your decorated project will seal the papier mâché and help protect it against damp. It will also enhance the colour in your painting, and preserve the detail. Polyurethane varnish is one of the best to use as it is so durable and easy to apply. It is available in both matte and gloss finishes – the choice is yours – but remember the type of varnish you choose will affect the look of the finished project.

Always varnish the entire surface, unless you intend to attach the item to some kind of backing, such as a wooden board. Polyurethane varnish does have a slight yellowing effect, which is not normally very noticeable, but if colour control is important you can use clear acrylic craft varnish or undiluted PVA medium.

Take your time when varnishing. Don't rush, just work methodically and evenly, particularly on larger projects – it's worth it in the end. Generally, each object will need five coats of varnish. Allow each layer to dry thoroughly as detailed on the manufacturer's instructions, before applying the next. Take care to wash out

your brushes thoroughly in a proprietary brush cleaner between coats of varnish as otherwise they will become rock hard and be completely unusable.

VARNISHING TOOLS
● Paintbrushes – about ½in (1.25cm) for general work
● Smaller paintbrush – for fine detail
● Polyurethane varnish – available in clear, matte or gloss

TIPS FOR PAINTING

● Practise new techniques and designs on some scrap paper first before decorating a papier mâché item

● If you are unhappy with your paint finish, leave for a while and return to it later. You may find you suddenly see the way to resolve a problem after coming back to it after a break. However, if you want to repaint an area, just apply a coat or two of white acrylic paint and start again.

BOWLS AND PLATES

1

2

3

4

MATERIALS
1 shallow bowl for mould
Petroleum jelly
Thinned PVA medium (see p. 9)
Flat-ended pasting brush
¾in (2cm) and 1in (2.5cm) newspaper strips (see p. 9)
Hair dryer (optional)
Kitchen paper
Lighter fuel (optional)
Scissors
Acrylic gesso
Various paintbrushes
Orange, red, yellow, green and blue drawing inks
Orange, red, green, blue and yellow poster paints
White acrylic paint
Polyurethane varnish

1 Choose a shallow bowl suitable to be a mould. Check that the bowl is clean and completely dry. Smear the outside of the upturned mould with petroleum jelly to act as a releasing agent.

2 Brush the thinned PVA medium onto the ¾in (2cm) newspaper strips with a flat-ended brush to cover the strips quickly and thoroughly. Apply eight layers of papier mâché – in alternate directions – following the method for layering papier mâché onto a mould (see p. 12). Leave the bowl aside to dry and harden for several hours between each layer. To accelerate the drying time of the papier mâché you can use a hair dryer for ten minutes at a time.

3 When the final layer of papier mâché is hard and dry, gently ease the bowl from the mould. Tear short chunks of newspaper about 1in (2.5cm) wide and apply two more layers of papier mâché around the rim to form a bold edge, and set aside to dry for several hours between layers.

4 Remove any residue of petroleum jelly with the kitchen paper. Gesso or any undercoat will not adhere to a greasy surface, and if any petroleum jelly remains it could lead to cracking and a breaking up of the finished decoration. Use lighter fuel to dissolve stubborn areas, if necessary. Then trim any rough edges with sharp scissors and apply the gesso undercoat evenly over the whole bowl. Decorate the bowl with the fruit pattern using the drawing inks, poster and acrylic paints. Finish the bowl with five coats of polyurethane varnish, leaving to dry between coats as detailed in the manufacturer's instructions.

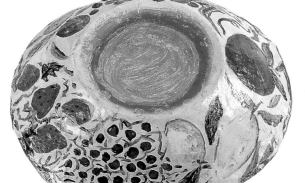

SUMMER BOWL

This decorative fruit bowl is simple to make, and can be filled with colourful fruit to liven up a side table.

The yellow ink background is painted onto the undercoat and contrasted with a red rim in poster paint. To make the pattern, paint summer fruits in orange, red, yellow, blue and green inks and poster paints onto the bowl. Leaves applied with colourful inks and paints inside the bowl can be muted with thinned white paint. Before this dries, remove some for a veiled effect.

BOWLS AND PLATES

MATERIALS

1 side plate for mould
Petroleum jelly
Thinned PVA medium (*see p. 9*)
Flat-ended pasting brush
¾in (2cm) newspaper strips (*see p. 9*)
Kitchen paper
Lighter fuel (optional)
Scissors
Various paintbrushes
Acrylic gesso
Red and green poster paints
Crimson and yellow drawing inks
White acrylic paint
Polyurethane varnish

1

2

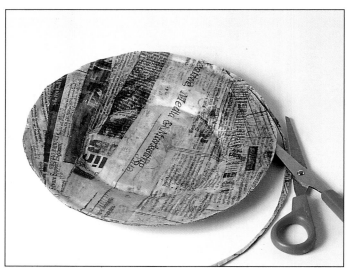

3

1 Prepare your mould by applying petroleum jelly as a releasing agent to the upturned side plate. Following the method for layering papier mâché onto a mould (*see p. 12*), apply the PVA to the newspaper with the flat-ended brush and lay strips across the mould, slightly overlapping each piece. When the side plate is completely covered by this first layer, set aside to dry for several hours.

2 Apply the second layer of strips across the first layer, but in the opposite direction. Apply eight layers of papier mâché in all, alternating the direction of the strips, and allowing each layer to dry for several hours before applying the next.

3 When the papier mâché is completely hard, carefully release the plate from the mould, and remove any residue of petroleum jelly with the kitchen paper or some lighter fuel, if necessary. Using sharp scissors trim away any newspaper ends around the rim to leave a neat, even edge. The plate is now ready for an undercoat of gesso over the entire surface. Decorate the plate with the spiral pattern using the poster and acrylic paints and drawing inks. Finally, finish with five coats of polyurethane varnish, leaving to dry between coats as detailed in the manufacturer's instructions .

SPIRAL PLATE

This side plate is ideal for beginners as it again uses the basic layered method. Once you've mastered the painting you can make several plates and use them for afternoon tea.

Take your time when applying the gesso undercoat to give an even surface on which to decorate. The paint technique uses several coloured layers. The top layer is partially scraped away to reveal the colours beneath.

The first layer is applied with red poster paint. When it is dry, deepen the effect by painting crimson ink over the plate. While this is still wet, use green poster paint to paint a bold spiral pattern from the centre of the plate out to the edge. Don't worry if the plate starts to look gaudy as the next stage tones down the colour. When the paint is dry, apply some undiluted white paint. Wait briefly, then smear with kitchen paper to remove some of this paint. Now pour some yellow ink onto the plate and rub in with fresh kitchen paper, scratching the painted surface through the paper to reveal the colour underneath.

1

2

3

4

MATERIALS
Modelling clay
Petroleum jelly
Cotton buds
Papier mâché pulp (see pp. 9–10)
Kitchen paper
Scissors
Acrylic gesso
Various paintbrushes
Red, yellow, orange, green and blue drawing inks
Brown, orange, green and blue poster paints
Polyurethane varnish

1 Roll out lengths of modelling clay into sausages about ⅝in (1.5cm) thick. Carefully coil the clay in a spiral, evenly bringing up the sides to create the pot shape – narrow at the bottom and wider at the top. Apply petroleum jelly as a releasing agent to the inside, using a cotton bud to get into the difficult, recessed areas of the coils.

2 Following the method for pulping papier mâché onto a mould (see p. 13), press a quantity of pulp inside the mould only to a depth of ¼in (6mm). Overlap the pulp at the rim of the mould to form

a lip. Allow the pulp to dry thoroughly for about a week. Then add another layer and again leave to dry until completely hard.

3 When the papier mâché is completely dry, carefully release it from the mould by unwinding the modelling clay from the outside of the pot. Remove any residue left by the petroleum jelly with kitchen paper and trim away rough edges around the bowl rim with the scissors.

4 Using a small clean brush, apply a coat of gesso evenly over the entire pot to give a smooth base coat

for decorating. Allow the gesso to dry thoroughly before you begin to decorate the pot in the rich terracotta colour. Then add the zig-zag or Aztec design using the drawing inks and poster paints. When the painting is complete, finish by applying five coats of polyurethane varnish, leaving to dry between coats as detailed in the manufacturer's instructions.

COIL POT

This simple pot design is based on the centuries-old tradition of coil pot making. It is decorated in a way that enhances its unusual, uneven exterior relief. When it is finished, fill the bowl with fruits or with scented potpourri to add a pleasant fragrance to a room.

The edge of the bowl needs to be trimmed carefully after releasing it from the mould. Don't expect perfect smooth curves as the real charm of the coil pot lies in its quirky simplicity, and the small irregularities that add to its "handmade" character.

To paint the pot, blend a rich terracotta brown using brown and orange poster paints plus red and yellow inks. Apply this carefully to the pot.

Take your time to decorate the exterior. It may take several coloured layers to produce a rich, earthy effect. Add fine lines for detail after the first layers have dried. Try applying different designs using zig-zag or Aztec patterns in orange, green and blue paints and inks to complement the relief areas. Practise your designs on paper first, before applying them to the pot.

LARGE DINNER PLATE

This stylish plate is perfect for serving mints or sweets to your guests after a dinner party. It can also be placed on a plate stand or in a show cabinet to make a striking home decoration.

To make your papier mâché plate, choose a dinner plate with a bold ridge on its base as a mould. This will make a distinct circular indentation toward the centre of the papier mâché plate from which the foil design radiates. Paint the finished plate in blue ink, followed by a coat of black poster paint brushed over the textured surface, to produce a lustrous midnight blue.

The pattern has been created with foil paper – it's worth remembering to save a few different types from chocolate bars and gift wrappings. Some foils are richly embossed and glossy, others have a matte finish and are more subdued. Silver paper will provide a sophisticated finish on the dark blue, background while bright foils lend a cheerful quality. Experiment with your design on scrap paper before committing yourself to the final effect.

1

2

3

4

MATERIALS
1 dinner plate for mould
Petroleum jelly
Cotton buds
Papier mâché pulp (see pp. 9–10)
Kitchen paper
Lighter fuel (optional)
Acrylic gesso
Various paintbrushes
Blue drawing ink
Black poster paint
Torn strips of foil paper
PVA medium
Polyurethane varnish

1 Select a dinner plate to use as a mould and carefully apply petroleum jelly as a releasing agent to the upturned plate. You can use a cotton bud, if necessary, to reach right into the recesses around the ridge of the plate on the base.

2 Apply the newspaper pulp to the plate, following the method for pulping papier mâché onto a mould (see p. 13), to a thickness of around ¼in (6mm). Leave the pulp to dry for about a week, then apply another layer to the same thickness. Again, leave to dry thoroughly for about the same amount of time.

3 The pulp must always be absolutely hard and dry before it can be released from the mould. Even slightly damp pulp will separate and stick to the mould if you attempt to try to release it before it has fully hardened. So gently remove the papier mâché and wipe away any residue of petroleum jelly with kitchen paper and lighter fuel, if necessary. Then apply the gesso with a paintbrush as an undercoat to the papier mâché plate.

4 Paint the finished plate with the blue ink, followed by a coat of black poster paint. When dry apply the torn strips of foil with PVA medium to the plate in your chosen pattern. Finish decorating the plate by applying five coats of polyurethane varnish, leaving to dry between coats as detailed in the manufacturer's instructions.

1

2

3

4

1 Select a large soup dish to act as a mould, one with a broad rim is ideal. Turn the dish upside down and smear on petroleum jelly, using a cotton bud to apply it to the ridge, if necessary. Apply a layer of papier mâché pulp to a thickness of about ¼in (6mm) to the mould, using the method for pulping papier mâché onto a mould (see p. 13). Leave the papier mâché to dry thoroughly for about a week.

2 Carefully release the mould when the papier mâché pulp is completely dry. Remove any residue of releasing agent from the dish with some kitchen paper or, if necessary, a little lighter fuel. Turn the dish upside down and, using the method for layering papier mâché onto a mould (see p. 12), apply three layers of newspaper squares with the PVA medium. Allow each layer to dry thoroughly for a few hours before applying the next one.

3 Once the last layer of papier mâché has hardened, turn the dish over and apply a layer of papier mâché pulp about ¼in (6mm) thick to the inside of the bowl. Trim away any excess of newspaper ends with scissors, and pulp over the rim edge.

4 When the process is complete and the dish is fully dry, apply an undercoat of gesso with a paintbrush over the entire surface. Decorate with the metallic paint, poster paint and inks to give a burnished metal effect. Finally, apply five coats of gloss varnish to the papier mâché dish, leaving to dry between coats as detailed in the manufacturer's instructions.

MATERIALS

1 large soup dish for mould
Petroleum jelly and cotton buds
Papier mâché pulp (see pp. 9–10)
Kitchen paper
Lighter fuel (optional)
Thinned PVA medium (see p. 9)
¾in (2cm) newspaper squares (see p. 9)
Scissors
Acrylic gesso
Various paintbrushes
Metallic bronze acrylic paint
Black poster paint
Gold metallic drawing ink
Gloss polyurethane varnish

METALLIC DISH

Papier mâché is the perfect medium to re-create many different effects and surfaces, including very convincing metallic finishes. This plate has been given a bronze metallic finish, making it particularly suitable at Christmas time to hold nuts or other seasonal fare.

Both the layered and pulp methods are used in this project to give the impression of raw, oxidized metal on the inside of the dish and a smooth, or polished effect on the outside. Here, the soup dish used for the mould has a slightly scalloped edge that gives an an uneven look to the interior surface, where the appearance is of lumpy, molten metal.

After the dish has been undercoated with gesso, apply metallic bronze acrylic paint, adding a lighter gold ink on top for extra colour variation. You can then roughly paint the inside with black poster paint to highlight the metal effect. Flick bronze acrylic paint with an old toothbrush onto the dish to produce a flecked finish, and add some neat blobs of bronze paint to exaggerate the metal-like texture.

FISH DISH

Here's a chance to develop your skills with modelling clay and make this highly individual fish dish. When it has been painted and varnished it makes a delightfully whimsical decoration that is perfect in the bathroom filled with shells, soaps or other bathroom goodies – although it won't survive submersion in the bath!

As you start to add strips of papier mâché to the tail, you will notice that the finer sculpted edges appear. Try and build on this technique to produce an elaborate, flowing tail. You will also need to apply two coats of gesso to give a really smooth surface to the fish, but be careful not apply any one coat too thickly as this might lead to unsightly cracking.

Dappled, pearlized acrylic paints in marine colours are the best to use to decorate the fish dish. First apply a base colour of blue or green poster paint to work on, then add layers of the blue and green pearlized paints and inks on top. When the last coat is dry, add fins, scales and an eye, using a mixture of red and green inks, white acrylic paint, purple and silver pearlized paints and red poster paint to give a luxuriant, shimmering effect to the finished dish.

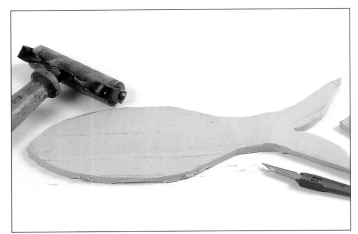

1

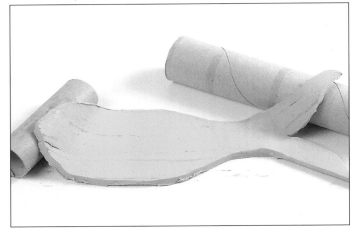

2

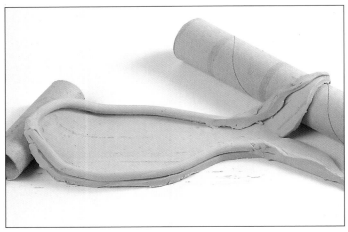

3

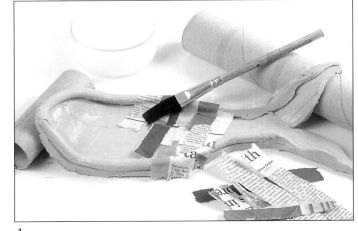

4

MATERIALS

Roller or rolling pin
Modelling clay
Craft knife
1 sheet of A4 paper and pen
Cardboard tubes
Petroleum jelly
Thin newspaper strips (*see p.* 9)
Thinned PVA medium (*see p.* 9)
Flat-ended pasting brush
Kitchen paper
Scissors
Acrylic gesso
Various paintbrushes
Blue or green and red poster paints
Purple, silver, blue and green pearlized paints; white acrylic paint
Red and green drawing inks
Polyurethane varnish

1 To form the mould for this fish dish roll out some modelling clay onto a suitable work surface. The clay should be about ¼in (6mm) thick, at least 12in (30cm) long and 6in (15cm) wide. Use a craft knife with a blunt blade to cut out a simple fish shape with flowing tail fins. If you are unhappy about cutting the clay freehand, use this photograph as guidance to draw a fish shape onto a piece of paper,

then blow it up to the required size on a photocopier. When you are satisfied with the result, cut out the template and place it over the modelling clay, so that it lies flat on the surface, then cut around it.

2 Lift the nose end of the fish and one of the tail fins to prop them onto the cardboard tubes. Adjust their angles several times so that they complement one another.

3 Roll out some modelling clay into long, thin sausages about ¼in (6mm) thick, and use them to build up a ridge on the outer edge of the fish mould, but leave the inner edges of the fin as they are. Smooth the joins with your finger.

4 Apply petroleum jelly as a releasing agent to the fish mould in readiness for the first layer of papier mâché strips.

5

6

7

8

5 Take the thin strips of newspaper and paste with the PVA medium and then, following the method for layering papier mâché onto a mould (*see p. 12*), apply eight layers to the dish. Remember to alternate the direction of each layer, and allow each one to dry for several hours before applying the next. The newspaper strips will also stick to the cardboard tubes, but this doesn't matter.

6 When the fish dish is completely dry, use a craft knife to help lever it from the mould. Remove any traces of the petroleum jelly with kitchen paper and trim away excess newspaper with scissors. Then carefully detach the cardboard tubes with scissors.

7 Turn the papier mâché fish over and apply another eight layers of newspaper strips to the underside

of the dish, as shown in the picture, alternating them as you proceed. Allow the strips to extend right over the ridge on the front side of the fish, and then neatly blend them in with your fingers. Again let each layer dry for several hours before applying the next.

8 When the papier mâché has completely hardened, trim away any rough pieces of newspaper with

the scissors to form an even edge. Then apply two coats of gesso as an undercoat, allowing it to dry thoroughly between coats, for a really smooth surface all over. Decorate the finished fish with the poster and pearlized paints and the drawing inks. Finally, when the paints are dry, apply five coats of polyurethane varnish, allowing to dry between coats as detailed in the manufacturer's instructions.

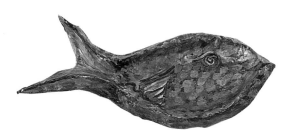

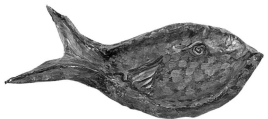

JEWELLERY

1

2

3

4

MATERIALS

Thinned PVA medium (see p. 9)

Flat-ended pasting brush

⅓in (10mm) newspaper strips
(see p. 9)

Scissors

Acrylic gesso

Various paintbrushes

Gold and silver metallic
acrylic paints

Gold and silver metallic
drawing inks

Black poster paint (optional)

Polyurethane varnish

Brooch fastener finding
(from art and craft stores)

Strong metal glue

1 This project uses newspaper strips and PVA medium to build up an intricate brooch, by twisting paper strips together in layers. Take about three newspaper strips and apply PVA medium along each strip with the flat-ended brush. Twist and fold each strip until half its original width. Repeat with three or four other strips of paper. Apply more PVA medium to the strips and start winding the first strip around itself to build up a papier mâché disc.

2 Continue to build up the brooch shape, adding more of the strips of twisted paper until you arrive at your chosen size. Set the papier mâché aside to dry – this may take at least one week at room temperature, since the newspaper gets very wet during the wrapping and twisting process. Try placing the brooch on a flat surface near a hot radiator to accelerate the drying time. Check from time to time that the brooch is staying flat, and press it firmly back into shape, if you find this is necessary.

3 Trim any excess newspaper away with sharp scissors and then apply a coat of gesso as an undercoat for the decoration. Paint this on with a small paintbrush, one side at a time. Gesso dries very quickly, so you will able to progress quite quickly now.

4 Decorate the brooch with layers of gold and silver metallic paint and ink. Rub a little black poster paint on too, if you want to give more of a "distressed" effect. Finish the brooch with five coats of varnish, leaving to dry between coats as detailed in the manufacturer's instructions. Finally, secure a brooch fastener onto the back of the brooch with strong glue and hold in place until it is firmly bonded.

TWISTED PAPER BROOCH

A simple design and an uncomplicated decorative treatment is used for this pretty brooch, which looks particularly attractive when pinned on dark, soft fabrics such as velvet.

The brooch can be made quite quickly; you just have to allow for drying time. You also need to make sure that when winding the twisted paper you have used enough PVA medium. If you apply too little, the paper will unravel or dry in an unstable condition. The tighter the paper is twisted together, the stronger and more durable the finished brooch will be. Several layers of metallic acrylic paints and inks are painted onto the brooch to create the rich gold and silver effect. You might also want to experiment with some different paint techniques. For a jazzier effect, try flicking fluorescent acrylic colours onto a dark base with an old toothbrush.

The technique of twisting layers of papier mâché used for the brooch can also be adapted to make some matching earrings that are very simple to make and great fun to wear.

BLACK AND GOLD BROOCH

Many papier mâché Victorian artefacts featured a mixture of black and gold paints to create an exotic and luxuriant effect when finished with lacquer. This project aims to emulate those Victorian finishes, using modern materials to achieve similar effects on a contemporary brooch design.

The brooch is quite straightforward to make, but when you start to paint on a coat of gesso, use a small brush and pay particular attention to the edges of the relief squares so that all the brooch is evenly covered.

A deep-black base colour is achieved by applying two coats of black poster paint, mixed with a little black Indian ink. Wait until the paint is completely dry, then draw geometric designs on the relief squares and apply a curving zig-zag pattern to the edge of the brooch. A gold metallic marker pen is particularly effective to use, although you may find that with some of these pens the design will fade slightly on varnishing (but you can touch up the pattern's detail once the varnish has dried). Alternatively, instead of using polyurethane varnish, apply five coats of undiluted PVA medium, as this is less likely to affect the design.

1

2

3

4

MATERIALS
1 bowl or cup for mould
Petroleum jelly
Thinned PVA medium (see p. 9)
Flat-ended pasting brush
1in (2.5cm) and ¼in (6mm) newspaper strips (see p. 9)
Kitchen paper
Lighter fuel (optional)
Scissors
Acrylic gesso
Various paintbrushes
Black Indian drawing ink
Black poster paint
Gold metallic ink marker pen
Polyurethane varnish or undiluted PVA medium
Brooch fastener finding
Strong glue

1 When choosing a mould suitable for this project, take time to select a bowl or cup with a pronounced ridge on the base. This will create a slight relief at the edge of the brooch that will accentuate the decoration of the brooch when it is painted. Apply petroleum jelly as a releasing agent to the base of the bowl, and about one-fifth of the way down the side. Paste the 1in (2.5cm) newspaper strips with the PVA medium and then apply, following the method for layering papier mâché onto a mould (see p. 12), to the base and top one-fifth of the mould, building up eight layers of strips. Leave to dry for several hours between layers.

2 Once the papier mâché has hardened, gently lift it from the mould. Remove any residue of petroleum jelly with some kitchen paper and a little lighter fuel, if necessary. Then, using a pair of sharp scissors, trim an even, curved edge about ⅝in (1.5cm) beyond the ridge of the brooch.

3 To make the relief pattern for the brooch, take the ¼in (6mm) newspaper strips, brush with some PVA medium and then fold into several squares. Continue to fold up the strips until they are the thickness of six layers of papier mâché. Leave all the squares to dry for about two to three days.

4 Arrange the squares on the brooch in an abstract design. When you have made an arrangement you like, glue them into place with the PVA medium. Apply a coat of gesso to the entire surface of the brooch with a fine brush. Decorate the brooch using ink, paint and a metallic marker pen. Apply five coats of either polyurethane varnish, leaving to dry between coats as detailed in the manufacturer's instructions, or PVA medium, leaving to dry for about a couple of hours between coats. Attach a brooch fastener finding to the back of the brooch with strong glue and hold in place for a minute or two to make sure that it has bonded firmly.

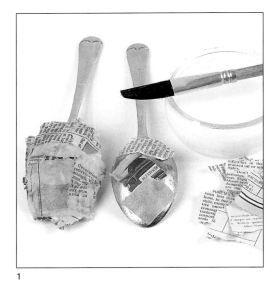

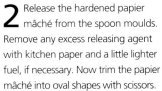

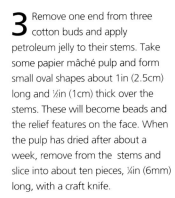

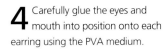

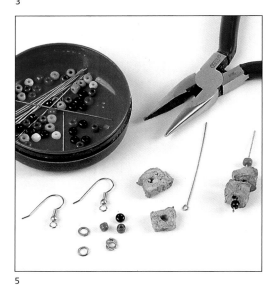

1 Take the two dessertspoon moulds. Smear petroleum jelly over the backs of the spoons to act as a releasing agent. Apply eight layers of the newspaper squares to the moulds with PVA medium, following the method for layering papier mâché onto a mould (*see p. 12*). Dry for several hours between layers.

2 Release the hardened papier mâché from the spoon moulds. Remove any excess releasing agent with kitchen paper and a little lighter fuel, if necessary. Now trim the papier mâché into oval shapes with scissors.

3 Remove one end from three cotton buds and apply petroleum jelly to their stems. Take some papier mâché pulp and form small oval shapes about 1in (2.5cm) long and ½in (1cm) thick over the stems. These will become beads and the relief features on the face. When the pulp has dried after about a week, remove from the stems and slice into about ten pieces, ¼in (6mm) long, with a craft knife.

4 Carefully glue the eyes and mouth into position onto each earring using the PVA medium.

5 Take the glass beads and plan your design with the pulp beads.

6 First check all the earring bits as shown. From the top you need: a pierced ear earring finding, a wire jewellery stem and jump rings to attach the stem to the face. Pierce a hole in each face with the craft knife to attach the jump rings. Then apply some gesso to the papier mâché parts. Decorate with paints and inks and later add five coats of polyurethane varnish, leaving to dry between coats as detailed in the manufacturer's instructions. Finally, assemble the earrings with pliers, bending the top of the stem to attach the finding and at the bottom to fix the jump ring.

MATERIALS

2 dessertspoons for moulds
Petroleum jelly
Thinned PVA medium (see p. 9)
Flat-ended pasting brush
Small squares of newspaper (see p. 9)
Kitchen paper
Lighter fuel (optional)
Scissors
Cotton buds for moulds
Papier mâché pulp (see pp. 9–10)
Craft knife
Red, blue and black glass beads (from craft stores)
Acrylic gesso
Various paintbrushes
Blue, purple, red and green poster paints
White pearlized acrylic paints
Black Indian drawing ink
Polyurethane varnish
Pliers, earring findings for pierced ears, wire jewellery stems and jump rings

EASY LEVEL

SPOON-FACE EARRINGS

Papier mâché is perfect for making hand-crafted jewellery, as even large earrings are light but very durable.

These dramatic earrings have been moulded onto spoons to create their shape and can be adapted to make different faces. They have been decorated with blue, purple, red and green poster paints, a touch of white pearlized paint, and black ink. Choose matching coloured glass beads to go on the earrings' stems.

The back of the face and the top pulp bead are painted in purple poster paint. The face is painted in blue to match the second glass bead; the mouth and the lower bead are painted red to complement the other pulp and glass bead, while the eyes are painted green. Apply some white pearlized paint all over the face to give a shimmering effect. For the face details use a fine paintbrush and black Indian ink.

By decorating the face's edge with black ink dashes you give it a mask-like quality. The dashes are complemented by stripes on the pulped beads.

1

2

3

4

1 Smear petroleum jelly over the back of the two dessertspoon moulds to act as a releasing agent. Apply eight layers of newspaper squares with the PVA medium onto the spoon backs, following the method for layering papier mâché onto a mould (*see p. 12*). Allow each layer to dry for several hours before adding another. When the papier mâché is hard, lift from moulds and remove any releasing agent with kitchen paper or lighter fuel, if necessary. Using sharp scissors cut a diamond shape from each piece of papier mâché about 2¼in (5.5cm) long and 1⅜ in (3.5 cm) wide.

2 Brush strips of newspaper ½in (1.3cm) wide with PVA medium. Remove one end from two cotton buds and smear petroleum jelly onto their stems, to act as a releasing agent. Wrap six layers of strips around the moulds to form some tubular beads. Fold two other strips into squares to a thickness of about six layers. Leave the beads and squares to dry thoroughly for about four to five days.

3 Using PVA medium attach a relief square of papier mâché to the middle of each diamond shape. Release the beads from the cotton-bud stems when they have completely hardened. Then apply a layer of gesso with a small brush to all four papier mâché earring components as an undercoat

4 Pierce a hole at least ¼in (6 mm) thick at the top of the diamond with the craft knife to insert a jump ring or wire and assemble the earrings. Then use poster paints, pearlized, paints, inks and pens to decorate the diamond shapes and tubular beads. Apply five layers of polyurethane varnish with a fine brush, leaving to dry between coats as detailed in the manufacturer's instructions, or alternatively use PVA medium, leaving to dry for a couple of hours between coats. Assemble the earrings as shown here from top to bottom, with the earring finding attached to the jewellery stem at the top. The black and green glass beads and papier mâché beads are threaded onto the stem and the stem is attached to the diamond shapes with jump rings. Use the pliers to bend and trim the stems into shape as necessary.

MATERIALS

Petroleum jelly

2 dessertspoons for moulds

Thinned PVA medium (*see p. 9*)

Flat-ended pasting brush

Small newspaper squares and
½in (1.3cm) strips (*see p. 9*)

Kitchen paper

Lighter fuel (optional)

Scissors

Cotton buds for moulds

Various paintbrushes

Acrylic gesso

Craft knife

Green and red poster paints

Green and gold pearlized
acrylic paints

Gold and crimson
drawing inks

Silver and gold metallic pens

Polyurethane varnish or
undiluted PVA medium

Earring findings for pierced
ears, wire jewellery stems and
jump rings, pliers

Black and green glass beads
(from craft stores)

EASY LEVEL

DIAMOND EARRINGS

These earrings are made in a similar way to the Spoon-Face Earrings (*see pp. 38–39*). Their subtle, but distinctive, decoration will really liven up a simple evening dress.

The base colour for the earrings is a deep bottle-green poster paint, visible only on the back. A light pearlized green acrylic paint is brushed over the front of the diamond and the beads, and the relief area is highlighted with gold pearlized acrylic paint and ink. When this is dry, rows of gold dots can be added on top with a metallic pen. The beads are decorated with a little gold paint, using quite a dry brush, to achieve the mottled effect.

The diamonds' borders are patterned with silver metallic pen dots with some crimson ink painted on top. Tiny flecks of deep-red poster paint, placed along the diamonds' borders and around the relief areas, help to contrast the green. The areas decorated with metallic pen can blur with normal varnish, so use undiluted PVA medium for a crisper finish.

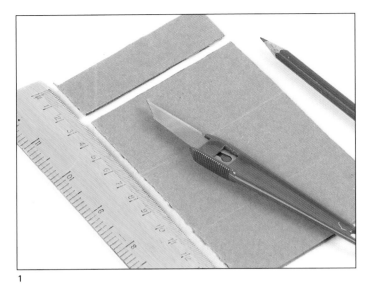

1

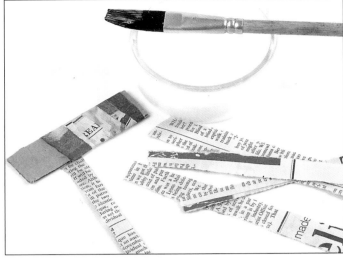

2

3

4

1 Use a craft knife and ruler to cut out a length of cardboard that is 3in x ¾in (7.5cm x 2cm) to form the base of the brooch.

2 Apply PVA medium to the newspaper strips with a flat-ended brush. Cover the card with five layers of papier mâché by wrapping the strips neatly around the card. Take extra care when applying the papier mâché strips to the ends of the card – this needs to be done evenly to make a neat and tidy finish. Leave the papier mâché strips to dry for several hours between each layer.

3 Brush the PVA medium all over the front surface of the brooch. Then take the string and press it into position on the brooch, curving it in a meandering design along the papier mâché as shown. Adjust the shape to suit your chosen design before the glue dries.

4 Once the PVA medium is dry, check that the string is firmly attached to the papier mâché. Trim away any excess string and then apply gesso to the entire surface with a small paintbrush. Decorate the brooch with poster paint, pearlized paints, metallic drawing inks and metallic pen. Then finish with five coats of polyurethane varnish, leaving to dry between coats as detailed in the manufacturer's instructions. To complete this piece of jewellery, attach a brooch fastener to the back of the brooch with strong glue for metal, holding it in place for a minute or two to make sure that you get a strong bonding.

MATERIALS

Craft knife
Ruler
Cardboard
Thinned PVA medium (*see p. 9*)
Flat-ended pasting brush
Thin newspaper strips (*see p. 9*)
String, 7in (17.5cm) long
Scissors
Acrylic gesso
Various paintbrushes
Purple poster paint
Green, blue, purple, pink and white pearlized paints
Cream, blue and violet metallic drawing inks
Silver metallic pen
Yellow, pink and blue drawing inks
Polyurethane varnish
Brooch fastener finding (from art and craft stores)
Strong glue

INTERMEDIATE LEVEL

STRING-LAYERED BROOCH

This brooch has a jewel-like appearance because of the shimmering effect of the painted dots. It looks good worn on both plain and textured fabrics.

The project shows you how to make exciting relief patterns on papier mâché objects. It shows a technique that can also be used very effectively on more ambitious projects, such as small bowls or large boxes.

To decorate the brooch, paint it in purple poster paint or, if preferred, black, navy blue or bottle green. Apply cream, blue and violet metallic inks, adding purple, green, blue, pink and white pearlized paints on top. Then use a fine brush to create dots and flashes of shimmering colour as seen in the two brooch styles above.

To create some highlights, add some flashes of silver with a metallic pen and then "wash" the brooch with layers of yellow, pink and blue inks to build up a really luxuriant sheen. Trace the string pattern with threads of the base colour and repeat this colour along the brooch's edges to finish.

43

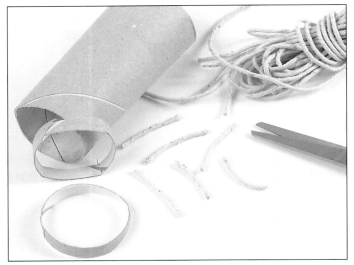

1

2

3

4

MATERIALS
Cardboard tubes
Ruler, scissors and string
Petroleum jelly and clingfilm
Papier mâché pulp (*see pp. 9–10*) and cotton buds
Acrylic gesso
Various paintbrushes
Turquoise, light-gold, pink pearlized acrylic paints
Black Indian drawing ink
Red poster paint
Polyurethane varnish
Craft knife and screw eyes
Wire jewellery stems, red and black glass beads, jump rings, earring findings, pliers

1 Using a cardboard tube, cut two sections measuring ⅜in (1cm) wide. Cut eight pieces of string that will fit snugly across the inside of the two tube discs.

2 Smear a little petroleum jelly onto some clingfilm and place the cardboard moulds on it. Make a star design using the pieces of string inside the moulds. The petroleum jelly will help keep the string in place.

3 Press the pulp tightly into the moulds, filling them right up to the top. Remove one end from two cotton buds and apply petroleum

jelly to the stems of two cotton buds, and with the papier mâché pulp mould a bead around each stem. Leave all the papier mâché pieces to dry thoroughly for about a week.

4 When the papier mâché medallions and beads are hard and dry, apply a coat of gesso to form an undercoat on all the surfaces. Then use the tip of the craft knife to make a small hole in the top of each medallion. Decorate the pieces with pearlized and poster paints and inks, and then varnish with five coats of polyurethane varnish, leaving to dry between coats

as detailed in the manufacturer's instructions. To finish the earrings, insert a screw eye into each of the earrings' holes. Then thread the glass and papier mâché beads all along the jewellery stem. Assemble the earrings by attaching the stem to the screw eye with a jump ring. Use pliers to bend the top of the wire stem to hook onto the earring findings, and then trim away excess wire with some sharp scissors.

CHUNKY EARRINGS

These bold, chunky earrings help you make a dress statement and are great fun to make. There's no need to worry about releasing them from the mould, as it forms part of the earring.

Papier mâché is often used to make theatrical props, as it is so lightweight, so heavy-looking jewellery can be produced easily using this technique. The earrings are painted in a light-gold pearlized acrylic paint as a base colour, with dabs of pink on top. Black Indian ink is then used to make bold stripes across the beads and on the edge of the earrings. Mix some black ink with the light gold to create a "distressed" effect on the string side of the earrings. You can then highlight the string and each earring's border with a turquoise pearlized paint, adding some spots of red poster paint to contrast with the background colour.

Red and black glass beads help to offset the rugged pulp bead on each stem. Alternatively, you can create an antique effect by painting the earrings in bronze and using gold beads.

AFRICAN BANGLE

Bright, vibrant and big, this bangle looks striking either worn on its own or with other bracelets. Decorated with bright, spicy colours, it can look good worn with a casual top or a more formal outfit.

The bangle can be finished with a smooth or rugged surface. To make a smooth finish, roll the pulped mould along a flat surface. For a rough effect, just leave the pulp in its natural state. After you have applied the gesso undercoat, paint the bangle in an earthy brown, orange or yellow base colour using poster paints. When this has dried you can add more decoration. Stripes or spots in spicy colours give the right look, as is shown in the two styles above. Paint them in gold and crimson ink and black and red paint over the earthy base colour to give a vibrant effect to each bangle.

Bear in mind that metallic inks are better finished with undiluted PVA medium to preserve the colours. However, metallic acrylic paint can be varnished normally.

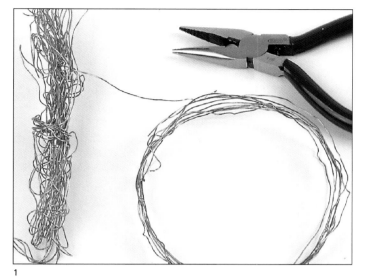

1

2

3

4

MATERIALS

Copper wire
(from hardware stores)

Papier mâché pulp
(*see pp. 9–10*)

Hair dryer (optional)

Acrylic gesso

Various paintbrushes

Red, black, brown, yellow
and orange poster paints

Gold and crimson drawing inks
or metallic acrylic paints,
if preferred

Undiluted PVA medium
or polyurethane varnish

1 Copper wire has been used in this project to form a structure for the pulp to be modelled around. Use your own arm as a measure for the size of the wire structure. Form a circle that has at least ⅜in (1cm) spare all round when drawn over your hand and comprises about eight strands of wire. Separate the wire strands slightly, and carefully secure ends together.

2 Using the papier mâché pulp, cover the wire structure until it forms a bangle that is about ¼in (2cm) thick. Roll the bangle along a flat surface, turning it around as you move it along, if you want to make all the sides smooth. If you prefer a bangle with a rough surface, simply let the pulp harden normally in its natural state.

3 Because of the thickness of the pulp, this project may well take up to two weeks to dry at room temperature. You can use a hair dryer to speed up the drying process, but don't attempt to heat the bangle in a microwave as its wire structure makes this method totally unsuitable. When the papier mâché is hard and dry, apply the gesso undercoat to the entire surface.

4 Decorate the bangle in bright colours with the poster paints and metallic inks. Finally, varnish with five coats of undiluted PVA medium, leaving to dry for a couple of hours between coats. Alternatively, if you want to use metallic paints, finish with five coats of the polyurethane varnish as normal, leaving to dry between coats as detailed in the manufacturer's instructions.

1

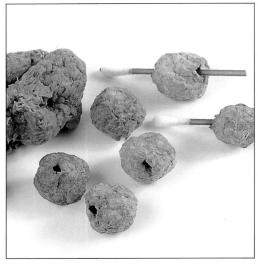

2

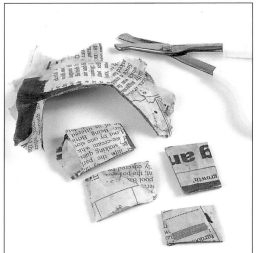

3

4

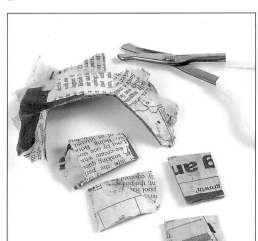

5

6

1 Make five round papier mâché pulp beads. Remove the ends from five cotton buds and apply petroleum jelly as a releasing agent to the stems. Roll a ball of pulp in the palm of your hand and push it onto one stem; repeat for the other four stems. Leave to dry for about a week.

2 The second bead used is a layered tubular bead. Prepare another six cotton buds in the same way as before. Apply PVA medium to the newspaper strips with a flat-ended brush. The technique used to produce these beads is easy: simply wrap the strips around the cotton bud stem, building up about six layers of newspaper. Leave to dry for four to five days.

3 The final bead is made from flat-layered papier mâché built up on the back of dessertspoons. Apply petroleum jelly as a releasing agent to the back of six spoons and then paste on the newspaper squares with PVA medium, following the method for layering papier mâché onto a mould (see p. 12). Build up eight layers, drying for several hours between layers.

4 When the papier mâché is hard, remove from the spoons. Then cut trapezoid shapes 1⅛in (3cm) x ¾in (2 cm) x 1⅛in (3cm) x ⅝in (1.5cm).

5 Brush more newspaper strips with PVA medium and tape the two halves of the bead together, using a cotton bud as a spacer.

6 Experiment with different designs for the beads by threading on a thong. Then remove them and apply a coat of gesso. Then decorate with the poster paints and finish each bead with five coats of polyurethane varnish, leaving to dry between coats as detailed in the manufacturer's instructions. Finally, thread the beads on a thong.

MATERIALS

MATERIALS
Papier mâché pulp (see pp. 9–10)
Petroleum jelly
Cotton buds
Thinned PVA medium (see p. 9)
Flat-ended pasting brush
¾in (2cm) newspaper strips and squares (see p. 9)
6 dessertspoons
Scissors
Leather thong (from craft stores)
Acrylic gesso
Various paintbrushes
Red, dark brown, green, light blue and yellow poster paints
Polyurethane varnish

ADVANCED LEVEL

AFRICAN BEAD NECKLACE

This bright, colourful necklace would look particularly good worn with T-shirts in bright, primary colours. It is assembled from three contrasting types of beads, and reflects the same ethnic theme as the African Bangle (*see pp. 46–47*). Once again vibrant poster colours have been used in various spot and stripe designs on a strong base colour: the round beads have been given a yellow base with dark-brown spots;

the tubular beads a dark-brown base with green stripes and the flat beads have a red base with yellow and blue stripes. When painting stripes onto the tubular beads, apply them in two sections, front then back, to avoid any smearing and blurring.

An easy way to varnish the beads is to thread each one onto the stem of a cotton bud, which is held upright in some modelling clay. You can then varnish them on both sides.

Once finished, the beads can be threaded onto a leather thong. To achieve other effects you might like to experiment with different types of boot laces, ribbon and the various strings found in hardware stores.

DECORATIONS

CHRISTMAS STAR

This bright star decoration is perfect to finish off a Christmas tree. A simple handmade mould and papier mâché pulp is all that is needed to make this easy decoration. You can, however, test your painting skills to produce intricate, colourful designs, or alternatively just keep it simple by applying a base coat of metallic silver paint and highlight with touches of gold as shown. Because the modelling-clay mould is not absolutely rigid, it will give a little when you press in the pulp. This helps to give the star a light, petal-like quality that will look fresh and bright among the Christmas greenery.

For the coloured star, paint one side red and one side yellow with poster paints and then apply some white acrylic paint to both sides. Then trace a shape around the edges of the centre star in bright green, yellow, blue, pink, and white poster or acrylic paints working outward. For a richly layered quality, add more flecks of the colours used.

You can also use this method to make large stars, which can be hung from the ceiling or fixed to the wall.

MATERIALS
Petroleum jelly and cling film
Modelling clay
Papier mâché pulp (see pp. 9–10)
Kitchen paper
Lighter fuel (optional)
Scissors
Acrylic gesso
Various paintbrushes
Silver and gold metallic acrylic paints
Green, white, yellow, red, blue and pink poster or acrylic paints
Polyurethane varnish
Craft knife
Screw eyes
Ribbon or hanging thread

1

2

3

4

1 Smear petroleum jelly as a releasing agent onto cling film. Cut five pieces of new modelling clay 4¾in (12cm) in length and ⅜in (1cm) wide. Use the "ribs" on modelling clay as guidance, the clay was cut at a width of two ribs. Form a star shape on the clingfilm by bending each piece of clay in half and joining it to the adjacent section. Make a simple star shape in the middle with clay one rib high, as shown.

2 Take the papier mâché pulp and press it into the star mould.

3 Leave the pulp to harden for about a week, before removing the modelling clay. Wipe away any residue of petroleum jelly with kitchen paper and some lighter fuel, if necessary. Trim, and then apply gesso to the star's surface.

4 Decorate the star using the metallic, poster or acrylic paints. Finish with five coats of polyurethane gloss varnish, leaving to dry between coats as detailed in the manufacturer's instructions. With a craft knife make a hole in the point at the top of the star and attach a screw eye. Thread a ribbon or thread through the hole so that you can hang it on the tree.

1

3

4

1 Using a marker pen and a ruler, draw two bow shapes about 5in (13cm) long and 2¾in (7cm) at the widest point onto cardboard, as shown above. Then neatly cut out the bows using a sharp craft knife and a ruler.

2 Take the papier mâché pulp and cover the facing side of the bow to a depth of about ¼in (6mm). When the pulp has hardened, after about a week, turn over and repeat the process on the other side, covering all remaining areas of cardboard. Then leave to dry for another week.

3 At the same time, make two triangular moulds from modelling clay: the larger one needs to be about 3¾in (8cm) at the sides by 2⅜in (6cm) at the base; the smaller triangle should be around 2in (5cm) at the sides by 1½in (4cm) at the base. Apply the petroleum jelly as a releasing agent to the clingfilm and place the moulds on top. Press papier mâché pulp into the moulds and then set them aside to dry for about a week.

4 When the papier mâché is completely hard, carefully remove the modelling-clay moulds.

Wipe off any residue of petroleum jelly with some kitchen paper and a little lighter fuel, if necessary. Apply an undercoat of gesso to the bows and triangles, leave to dry, then decorate with the poster, pearlized or acrylic paints and the metallic inks. Finally, varnish with five coats of undiluted PVA medium, leaving to dry for a couple of hours between coats. To complete the project, attach screw eyes to the bows and triangles to link them together. You can then thread some silver string or ribbon through the eyes so that you can hang the bows on the Christmas tree, or as a ceiling decoration.

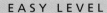

CHRISTMAS BOWS

This string of decorations has been inspired by traditional Christmas bows. Painted in blues and acid yellows, rather than the traditional green and red, they have a sparkling and seasonal look to them and make a fresh and lively alternative to mass-produced, shop-bought decorations.

The simplified bows are decorated in bands of purple, dark-blue, light-blue and black poster paints and ink. After this layer has dried, more detail can be applied using a light-blue pearlized paint and silver metallic ink to add that extra sparkle.

The triangular shapes are painted in a base coat of acid-yellow poster paint, followed by bold dashes of black Indian ink around the edges. A black shape is then painted in the centre of the triangles. Spot a little light-blue pearlized colour on as a final paint layer, before varnishing with PVA medium. Buy some silver string or ribbon to thread this decoration and then hang the bows on the Christmas tree, or alternatively on the wall.

MATERIALS

Marker pen
Ruler
Cardboard
Craft knife
Papier mâché pulp (*see pp. 9–10*)
Modelling clay
Clingfilm
Petroleum jelly
Kitchen paper
Lighter fuel (optional)
Acrylic gesso
Various paintbrushes
Yellow, purple, dark-blue, light-blue and black poster paints
Light-blue pearlized acrylic paints
Black Indian and silver metallic drawing inks
Undiluted PVA medium
Screw eyes
Silver string or ribbon

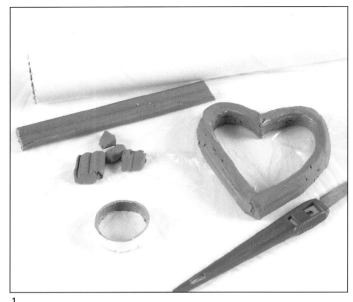

1

2

3

4

1 The decorations in this project are formed in three different ways: two use moulds, while the third is modelled "freehand" in papier mâché pulp. To make the moulds, use a craft knife to cut two lengths of modelling clay about 5½in (14cm) long and ⅜in (1cm) wide and model together to form a suitable heart shape. Cut a disc from a cardboard tube about ¼in (6mm) wide. Apply some petroleum jelly to the clingfilm to act as a releasing agent and then place both the bow moulds on top of this surface.

2 Press papier mâché pulp into the moulds and set aside to dry for about a week.

3 Use your modelling skills to form a smaller heart from the papier mâché pulp directly onto the cling film. Keep adjusting the shape until you are happy with your heart, then leave to dry as Step 2.

4 Release the papier mâché from the moulds, trim, and remove any residue left by the petroleum jelly with kitchen paper and a little lighter fuel, if necessary. Apply gesso as an undercoat to all the papier mâché surfaces and decorate using poster paints and metallic ink. Varnish with five coats of undiluted PVA medium, leaving to dry for a couple of hours between coats. Attach the screw eyes as shown, and thread on all the pieces using the silver string or cord.

MATERIALS

Craft knife

Modelling clay

Cardboard tube

Clingfilm

Petroleum jelly

Papier mâché pulp
(*see pp. 9–10*)

Scissors

Kitchen paper

Lighter fuel (optional)

Acrylic gesso

Various paintbrushes

Red and blue poster paints

Silver metallic ink

Undiluted PVA medium

Screw eyes

Silver string or cord

EASY LEVEL

CHRISTMAS HEARTS

This pretty Christmas heart decoration looks good on the Christmas tree or hanging on its own. It can be made quite quickly and gives beginners a chance to model papier mâché pulp without using a mould. Simple decorations often look the best, and with this in mind, the colour scheme that is painted on this decoration is deliberately restrained.

The surface on the pulped hearts is quite rugged and you may prefer to create a smoother surface. To do this, rub down the rough surfaces with a nail file, fill with wood filler, leave to dry, then smooth with sandpaper.

Basically, the two hearts and the circular disc decorations are painted in either silver ink or red poster paint, with all their edges outlined in a rich blue poster paint.

1

2

3

4

MATERIALS

Petroleum jelly
Avocado stone or similar as a mould
Modelling clay
Papier mâché pulp (see pp. 9–10)
Cotton buds
Kitchen paper
Lighter fuel (optional)
Acrylic gesso
Various paintbrushes
Yellow poster paint
Blue, red and green and gold metallic (optional) drawing inks
White acrylic paint; gold metallic acrylic paint
Undiluted PVA medium or polyurethane varnish
Screw eyes
Red glass beads
Nylon thread and needle
Strong glue
Scissors
Ribbon

1 To make one bell, prop the avocado stone, pointed end up, in modelling clay to hold it steady. Then apply petroleum jelly as a releasing agent to about three-quarters of the stone.

2 Take the papier mâché pulp and cover three-quarters of the stone with pulp to a depth of at least ¼in (6mm). Remove the ends from three cotton-bud stems and apply petroleum jelly as a releasing agent. Form papier mâché pulp beads by rolling the pulp in a ball and inserting the stems through the centre. Leave the beads to dry for about a week.

3 When the papier mâché is fully hardened, carefully remove it from the moulds. Wipe away any residue of petroleum jelly from the inside of the bell shape, using some kitchen paper and a little lighter fuel, if necessary.

4 Apply gesso as an undercoat to all the papier mâché surfaces. Decorate with the poster paint and inks. If metallic inks have been used, varnish with five coats of PVA medium, leaving to dry for a couple of hours between coats. If metallic inks have not been used, apply five coats of polyurethane varnish and

leave to dry between coats as detailed in the manufacturer's instructions. Then attach a screw eye into the top of the bell. Next, place a glass bead onto a length of nylon thread. Thread both ends together through the eye of a needle and feed on a pulp bead. Use the needle to pierce a hole at the top of the bell, and pull through from the inside to the outside. Knot both ends of the thread to the screw eye and reinforce with some glue. Trim the thread, and then put a colourful ribbon through the screw eye of the bell and hang on the tree. Make other bells in the same way.

CHRISTMAS BELLS

Make an interesting addition to your festive decorations with these pretty Christmas bells that have been modelled in the style of painted Russian crafts. Cluster several together to display on a wreath, place with foliage as a table decoration, or hang on the Christmas tree – whichever way the bells are presented they will look seasonal and jolly. To ensure an exact colour match, it is a good idea to paint each bell and bead at the same time. Paint each bell and bead with a bright base colour, such as yellow poster paint. When applying the ring of colour at the base of the bell, brush the paint on with small downward strokes. A little of the paint will spray from the edge of the bell and produce a subtle speckling on the inside surface. Then paint the bell in white acrylic paint to cover two-thirds of the bell, working downward, and use this as a base to paint simple designs in blue, red and green ink. Finally, decorate each of the bells with a band of gold paint or ink.

1

2

3

4

MATERIALS
Modelling clay
Petroleum jelly
Papier mâché pulp (see pp. 9–10)
Craft knife
Acrylic gesso
Various paintbrushes
Black drawing ink
Brown, yellow, red, green and fawn poster paints
White, black and metallic bronze acrylic paint
Light-gold pearlized paint
Polyurethane varnish
Screw eyes
Red cord or ribbon

1 Roll a piece of modelling clay into a ball and gently form the shape of a bird's head and tail. Smooth the modelling clay and make the slight suggestion of wings at the side, as shown.

2 Apply petroleum jelly as a releasing agent to the whole mould. Following the method for pulping papier mâché onto a mould (see p. 13), cover the bird to a depth of about ¼in (6mm), leaving an opening on the base. Allow the papier mâché to dry for about a week, and build up with more pulp, then leave to dry again.

3 When the pulp has fully hardened, gently remove the modelling clay through the base with the help of a craft knife. Squash a little bit of pulp in your hands and patch over the opening, then put the model aside to dry thoroughly for a few days.

4 Apply an undercoat of gesso to the entire surface of the bird. Then paint the plumage and pear-tree design onto the model, following the design shown opposite, with the poster, acrylic, metallic and pearlized paints and ink. Apply five coats of polyurethane

varnish to the bird, leaving to dry between coats as detailed in the manufacturer's instructions. Finally, if you intend to use the project as a hanging decoration, attach a screw eye halfway along the bird's back and thread on some red cord. Alternatively, leave it as it is and place it on a shelf or table with a mixture of other Christmas decorations.

PARTRIDGE IN A PEAR TREE

This project is based on the first gift that is sent in the song: "The Twelve Days of Christmas" – a partridge in a pear tree. Children will love this bird, who sits so cheerfully in the Christmas foliage.

Modelled over a handmade mould, each bird will vary. You may well be surprised at how the pulp shrinks, but another layer can always be added. To create the effect of the partridge sitting in a pear tree, the lower part of the model has been painted with pears and foliage. Start by painting the pears in a yellow poster paint, outlining them in a little red, so that they stand out clearly against the green leaves. Use a fine paintbrush, and paint in layers to give extra detail.

To create the plumage and the bird's face, use dashes of brown, yellow and fawn poster paint, and then add more detail on the feathers with black ink and bronze metallic paint. Use light-gold pearlized paint to give a shimmering effect, plus dabs of white acrylic paint for highlights. Define the eyes, beak and tail in black acrylic paint.

SNOWMAN

The final Christmas decoration in this section is a jolly snowman character. It can be popped in as an extra stocking filler for the children, hung with the other decorations on the Christmas tree or it can be used as the centrepiece for a children's Christmas party.

The snowman wears a football scarf as well as a hat, and the team colours are your choice. The texture of the pulp gives the snowman a very convincing snow-like quality, a feature that is worth taking advantage of when building up the second layer of papier mâché pulp.

As the snowman is already painted white from his coat of gesso, there is no need on this occasion to apply a base colour. Use orange, black, green, red and blue poster paints or acrylic paints to decorate the hat, scarf and carrot nose. Black Indian ink mixed with black poster paint makes a satisfying, deep jet-black colour that is perfect for emphasizing the coal buttons, eyes and mouth. To retain the snowman's fresh white look, varnish with five coats of undiluted PVA medium.

1

2

3

4

MATERIALS
Modelling clay
Petroleum jelly
Papier mâché pulp (see pp. 9–10)
Craft knife
Acrylic gesso
Various paintbrushes
Orange, black, green, red and blue poster or acrylic paints
Black Indian ink
Undiluted PVA medium
Screw eyes
Nylon thread or ribbon

1 Use modelling clay to form a stout body for the snowman mould. Roll a small piece into a ball and attach firmly to the body as a head. Smooth over any joins and stretch out the neck a little. Form a hat and small arms from the modelling clay and attach them to the head and body. Apply petroleum jelly to act as a releasing agent to the whole of the model.

2 Following the method for pulping papier mâché onto a mould (see p. 13), cover the snowman mould to a depth of about ¼in (6mm). Leave an opening at the base of the mould free from pulp. Form details from pulp, such as buttons, eyes and a carrot nose, and press them firmly into the wet pulp.

3 Allow the papier mâché to dry for about a week, then add more pulp to build up the brim of the hat and fatten out the body, if necessary. Leave to dry as before. When all of these areas have hardened, remove the modelling-clay mould with the help of a craft knife through the opening at the base. Squash a little pulp in your hand and patch over the opening. Set aside to dry for a few days.

4 Apply an undercoat of gesso to the model and it will immediately take on its snowman appearance. Use bright poster or acrylic paints and ink to decorate, and finish with five coats of PVA medium, leaving to dry for a couple of hours between coats. If you intend to hang up the decoration, insert a screw eye through the top of the snowman's hat, and attach thread or ribbon through this.

MATERIALS

Cardboard
Marker pen
1 side plate (optional)
1 sheet of A4 paper (optional)
Scissors
Craft knife
Papier mâché pulp (see pp. 9–10)
Thinned PVA medium (see p. 9)
Flat-ended pasting brush
Oblong pieces of newspaper (see p. 9)
Acrylic gesso
Various paintbrushes
Blue ink
Blue, purple-blue poster paints
Light-blue and violet pearlized acrylic paints
Silver metallic pen
Polyurethane varnish
Screw eye
Nylon thread or ribbon

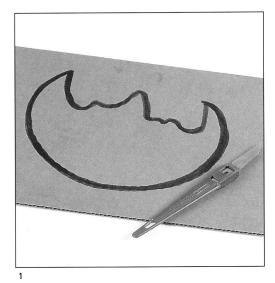

1

2

3

4

1 Draw the pattern of a half moon with a profiled face onto a piece of cardboard with a marker pen. If you are unsure about drawing freehand straight onto the card, follow this simple method for a template. Place a side plate upside down on a sheet of A4 paper and then draw around it. Remove the plate and, using the picture for guidance, sketch in the moon face profile, elongating the nose and chin. Cut out the template and use it to draw around on the cardboard. Use a sharp craft knife to cut out the moon shape, taking care to cut away from yourself.

2 Following the method for pulping papier mâché onto a mould (see p. 13), cover the front of the cardboard to build up the moon's facial features and develop the curved edge into a crescent moon. Set aside and allow the pulp to harden for about a week.

3 When the pulp is dry, turn the moon model over and paste the newspaper pieces with PVA medium. Apply five layers, using the method for layering papier mâché onto a mould (see p. 12). Don't worry if the newspaper pieces overlap the edge of the cardboard.

4 Wait until the model is dry before you trim excess newspaper from the cardboard. Neaten the moon's edges with papier mâché pulp and continue to build up the features on the moon. Set aside to dry for a few days, then apply a coat of gesso. When dry, decorate with the ink, poster and pearlized paints and pen. Finish with five coats of polyurethane varnish, leaving to dry between coats as detailed in the manufacturer's instructions. Attach a screw eye at the top of the moon and paint with pearlized paints to match the decoration. Hang the moon with nylon thread or ribbon.

HANGING MOON

A moon is a magical, evocative image that has been represented in story books and pictures for centuries. The hanging moon in this project is based on a crescent moon with a typical man-in-the-moon profile.

Use your modelling skills to build up the relief on the moon's exaggerated features and its sloping edges. To decorate the moon, use several shades of blue to paint the moon in a really deep, shimmering night-sky colour. To make the base colour, mix blue ink and blue poster paint together, then apply this blend to the surface of the moon. A dark purple-blue paint is then useful to accentuate the relief areas around the facial features. Finally, use some light-blue and violet pearlized paints to create some floating cloud effects all around the moon.

Paint flecks of silver paint onto the face to represent passing stars, then brush more blue ink over the top for a veiled effect. Hang your moon up with some papier mâché stars (*see pp. 52–53*), or maybe place it by a window where a light breeze may catch it.

1

2

3

4

5

6

1 Apply petroleum jelly to act as a releasing agent to the top side of your saucer mould. Paste the newspaper strips with PVA medium and, following the method for layering papier mâché onto a mould (*see p. 12*), apply eight layers of strips in alternate directions. Leave to dry for several hours between layers.

2 Once the papier mâché has hardened, release it from the mould. Remove any residue of petroleum jelly using kitchen paper and a little lighter fuel, if necessary. Trim the edge of the papier mâché for an even-shaped base.

3 Take some papier mâché pulp and form a ball to make a face. Flatten the ball to a thickness of ¼in (6mm) and apply to the centre of the base. Roll tiny sausages of pulp to form the nose, eyebrows and mouth. Use small pulp balls to form the cheeks and eyes. Roll larger chunks of pulp into sausages to make rays of sun to radiate out from the face. Pinch the centre of the rays upward to form an interesting relief, and press the base of the rays firmly into place.

4 As you add more rays, the radius of the face starts to increase. Smooth the edges of the relief areas with your finger and add more details as necessary. Leave to dry for about a week.

5 Trim sun shape and apply gesso as an undercoat, using a fine paintbrush on the detailed areas.

6 Apply the base ink straight onto the gesso, then add the poster and acrylic paints and more inks. Finish with five coats of polyurethane varnish, leaving to dry between coats as detailed in the manufacturer's instructions. Attach a screw eye into the top of the sun and reinforce with glue. Hang the sun from nylon thread.

HANGING SUN

This sun looks at its best when it is displayed in natural light in a window or conservatory, for example.

Making the sun itself provides a more challenging opportunity for you to practise your modelling skills than some of the previous projects. You can make several suns and each one can convey different moods and characteristics: one can have a fiery expression, another a sad face and a third a warm, beaming smile. Explore all these possibilities with the face when you are modelling the pulp and later on when

you decorate it. Generally, it works best to use a sunshine yellow ink as a base as inks give such a strong colour. The ink also accumulates in the crevices of the relief, giving it an attractive, translucent appearance. Add some red and gold inks onto the base coat, create some highlights with white acrylic paint, and then mix in some yellow, orange and red poster and acrylic paints to give greater definition to the sun's face.

Don't forget to paint the reverse side of the sun too, as this is a free hanging object and both sides will be seen.

If you want to achieve a sun that really glows, just paint it in a gold or bronze metallic paint. To make a much larger sun, use a serving plate, or circular tray as the base mould.

MATERIALS

1 large saucer for mould
Petroleum jelly, thinned PVA medium (see p. 9)
Flat-ended pasting brush
1in (2.5cm) newspaper strips, (see p. 9), kitchen paper
Lighter fuel (optional), scissors
Papier mâché pulp (see pp. 9–10)
Acrylic gesso
Various paintbrushes
Red, gold and yellow inks
Red, orange and yellow poster paints
White, red, orange, yellow plus gold or bronze metallic acrylic paints
Polyurethane varnish
Screw eye, glue, nylon thread

ADAM AND EVE WALL PLAQUE

The spectacular relief modelling on this wall plaque depicts the story of Adam and Eve in the Garden of Eden. With its strong colours it can make a dramatic hanging picture against a plain background. Allow yourself plenty of time to model the figures, adding extra pulp to produce finer details after the first layer has dried. The roughly applied papier-mâché base is an ideal background on which to paint exotic flowers and foliage.

Define the skyline, somewhere above the top of the heads of the two figures, and paint in blue poster paint, then use some white and bright-blue pearlized paint and blue inks to depict this area. Paint the remaining background in lively jungle-green poster paint and ink and decorate with colourful plants on top. The Adam and Eve characters are painted in brown poster paint and gold pearlized paint to contrast with the purple/pinky colour of the snake and also the brightly coloured red fruit. Highlight the tree with some orange and yellow poster paint.

Use inks to accentuate the colours, plus a little black ink to define the various features and to add to the striking effect of this tableau. The edges of the plaque turn upward, so decorate the reverse side in a base colour that has already been used on the front, such as green or blue.

1

2

3

4

MATERIALS
1 baking tray for mould
Clingfilm and petroleum jelly
2 double newspaper sheets, PVA medium, bucket, hair dryer
Kitchen paper
Papier mâché pulp (see pp. 9–10)
Acrylic gesso
Various paintbrushes
Blue, green, red, brown, orange and yellow poster paints
Blue, purple, light-gold, pink and white pearlized acrylic paints
Black, blue, red, yellow and green inks
Polyurethane varnish
Craft knife, leather thong

1 Cover the top surface of the baking tray with clingfilm and smear it with petroleum jelly to act as a releasing agent.

2 Take the newspaper sheets, tear into 16 pieces, and soak well in the PVA medium in a bucket.

3 Remove the first piece of newspaper from the bucket and squeeze out any excess solution. Scrunch up the newspaper and place it on the mould, squashing it down firmly with your hand. Repeat this process with the next piece, making sure it overlaps the first. Continue in this manner until the entire mould inside the metal ridge of the tray is covered with the newspaper pieces. Leave the papier mâché to harden. This may take a while, possibly a week or two, but the process can also be speeded up by using a hair dryer for periods of up to ten minutes at a time.

4 When the papier mâché has completely hardened, lift it from the mould and carefully peel off the clingfilm. Remove any residue of petroleum jelly with some kitchen paper. The base section for the plaque is now complete.

5

6

7

8

5 Taking the papier mâché pulp, form a tree shape by rolling it into sausages of pulp for the trunk and branches. Flatten them out as you secure them to the papier mâché base, then apply smaller pieces of pulp to form the apple shapes on the tree.

6 To make the snake that is coiled up the trunk of the tree, roll some small sausages of pulp and then press them lightly onto the trunk at an oblique angle. Form the snake's head with your fingers, so that it appears on the lowest branch of the tree.

7 Using the picture for guidance, model the pulp to form the Eve character reaching up for an apple next to the snake's head. The easiest way to construct a human body in relief form is to make up the basic frame of the body in sausages of pulp for the torso and limbs. A ball of pulp can then be used for the head. Press the pulp to mould the details of the figure and head.

8 Finally, construct the figure of Adam standing on the other side of the tree from Eve. Use the same basic method as before, but simply change the details as shown.

The plaque will take some weeks to dry at room temperature, as the layered base tends to absorb a lot of moisture from the pulp relief. Allow it to harden fully before applying an undercoat of gesso, then decorate with the brightly coloured poster and pearlized paints and inks. Finish the plaque with five coats of polyurethane varnish, leaving to dry between coats as detailed in the manufacturer's instructions. To complete, cut two holes with a sharp craft knife at either side of the plaque and attach a leather thong through the holes. Tie the ends together and hang on the wall.

1

2

MATERIALS

Oval-shaped party balloon
Marker pen
Bucket or bowl
Masking tape
Petroleum jelly
Papier mâché pulp (see pp. 9–10)
Kitchen paper
Lighter fuel (optional)
Acrylic gesso
Various paintbrushes
Red and black poster paints
Gold metallic acrylic paint
Light-gold, pink and blue pearlized acrylic paints
Red and black drawing inks
Polyurethane varnish
Craft knife
Red ribbon

3

4

1 This mask is moulded onto a party balloon. Blow up the balloon and draw a devil face – complete with horns – onto it with a marker pen. Prop the balloon in a bucket or bowl with the devil facing upwards, lying as flat as possible, and secure in place with some masking tape. Apply petroleum jelly to act as a releasing agent to the area to be covered by papier mâché.

2 Following the method for pulping papier mâché onto a mould, cover the area drawn on the mask to a minimum depth of ¼in (6mm). Model a pointed nose and chin, and then make ridges above the eyes to accentuate the shape of the devil's eyebrows. Leave the papier mâché pulp to harden on the mould for about a week.

3 When the papier mâché has fully dried, remove the balloon carefully. Use more pulp to reinforce any weak points on the first layer of papier mâché, and add any further details to the mask face. Then leave to dry again for about a week.

4 When the second application of pulp has hardened, remove any residue of petroleum jelly with kitchen paper and a little lighter fuel, if necessary. Apply a coat of gesso over the the mask and decorate with poster, metallic and pearlized acrylic paints and inks. Seal the mask with five coats of polyurethane varnish, leaving to dry between coats as detailed in the manufacturer's instructions. Use a craft knife to make an incision on the lower area of each ear. Thread a piece of red ribbon through each side and tie in place.

DEVIL MASK

A mask made from papier mâché is extremely light to wear, but because the material is remarkably strong it is very difficult to damage, and is therefore suitable even when children's games get rather boisterous.

The style of this devil's mask is based on a very simple mould, and the features can be modelled to be as hideous and frightening as you like! It is decorated in colours associated with the

devil – red, black and a dull gold, painted in blocks of poster, acrylic and pearlized paints and inks. To highlight the mask and create some extra interest, add dabs of the light gold, pink and blue pearlized paints. If you are looking for inspiration on how to decorate your mask, try the reference section of your local library as it often has books on different types of masks that are worn in tribal cultures abroad.

When the mask is finished, attach ribbons through holes in each side so that it can be firmly attached to a child's face. Alternatively, the mask can make an effective wall hanging at Halloween, or be worn for a party.

DECORATIONS

MATERIALS

Oval-shaped party balloon
Marker pen
Bucket or bowl
Masking tape
Petroleum Jelly
Papier mâché pulp (see pp. 9–10)
Thinned PVA medium (see p. 9)
Flat-ended pasting brush
¾in (2cm) strips of white tissue paper
Kitchen paper
Lighter fuel (optional)
Acrylic gesso
Various paintbrushes
White acrylic paint
Pink, red, blue drawing inks; gold and silver metallic drawing inks
Light-gold and white pearlized acrylic paints
Matt polyurethane varnish or undiluted PVA medium
Craft knife
Gold ribbon

1

2

3

4

1 Blow the balloon up and, as shown, draw an outline of a cherub face with wings using a marker pen. Prop the balloon in a bucket or bowl with the cherub facing upward, lying as flat as possible, and secure in place with masking tape. Apply petroleum jelly to act as a releasing agent to the area to be covered by papier mâché.

2 Following the method for pulping papier mâché onto a mould (see p. 13), cover the area mapped out on the balloon to a minimum depth of ¼in (6mm). Model the cherub's lips and soft, rounded features, plus its curly locks and wings. Leave the pulp to harden on the balloon for about a week. Then add in any further detail that is necessary using more pulp. Leave to dry again for a further week.

3 When the second application of papier mâché pulp has completely dried, carefully release the mask from the mould. Remove any residue of petroleum jelly with kitchen paper and a little lighter fuel, if necessary. Paste PVA solution onto the tissue paper strips and apply to the facial area of the mask. Build up the tissue paper to three layers to produce a really smooth finish. Leave the paper to dry for about an hour between each layer.

4 Apply an undercoat of gesso. When dry, decorate the cherub mask with pearlized, metallic and acrylic paints and metallic inks.

Finally, apply five layers of matte polyurethane varnish, leaving to dry between coats as detailed in the manufacturer's instructions. Or you can use PVA medium to finish, leaving to dry for a couple of hours between coats. When the last coat of varnish is dry, use a sharp craft knife to make a small incision to the lower wing area on each side of the mask. Thread a piece of gold ribbon through each hole and then secure each one firmly in place by using a strong knot.

CHERUB MASK

The most unusual aspect of this cherub mask is the smooth paper finish on the face, which is in marked contrast to the style of the Devil Mask (*see pp. 72–73*) with its intentionally rather rugged texture.

To create a slightly translucent effect on the tissue-paper finish, brush a light coat of diluted white acrylic paint over the tissue and then use a minute quantity of pink ink to give the cherub some rosy cheeks. The eyes are highlighted in blue ink and the lips are painted with a bright red ink, but still maintain a delicate, pastel appearance. The wings and hair have been decorated with the gold, white and silver pearlized and metallic inks to emphasize the angel look.

By coating the mask in a matte polyurethane varnish or PVA medium you give it a softer, almost ethereal quality. Attach two pieces of gold ribbon to the cherub, so that it can be used as a mask at Christmas time, or for fancy dress parties. Alternatively, it can be hung on a wall to make a charming decoration.

1

2

3

4

1 Place a large handful of the papier mâché pulp into an old plastic container. Add the red drawing ink to the pulp and mix together thoroughly. Add more of the ink to the pulp if you feel you want to achieve a stronger, deeper shade of red.

2 Place a sheet of cling film on a work surface, smear a little petroleum jelly onto it as a releasing agent, and then model two heart shapes, about ¼in (6mm) thick, from the papier mâché pulp. Set the hearts aside to dry thoroughly for about a week.

3 Fold in half a sheet of A4-sized thin white card. Remove the papier mâché hearts from the clingfilm and position them around the card. Keep moving them to different places until you are completely happy with the arrangement of your finished design. Then use a pencil to trace around the hearts to mark their final location.

4 Take off the hearts and paint your valentine design onto the card using the poster paints, inks and metallic pen. Take care not to saturate the card with too much paint or ink as this will spoil it

causing it to warp and wrinkle. When you are satisfied with your painted design, take the papier mâché hearts and fix them in position with some PVA medium. You can then write your special message to your valentine inside the card with the silver metallic pen.

EASY LEVEL

VALENTINE CARD

Everyone appreciates receiving a hand-made greetings card, and the personal touch takes on a romantic aspect when the card takes the form of a valentine.

By dying the pulp with red ink, rather than applying paint and varnish as normal, the papier mâché has a subtle, soft appearance. Use thin card, rather than stiff paper, that will stand up on its own. Many stationers and art stores sell card cut to A4 size, sometimes in packs specifically for people to make homemade cards.

You may like to practise your design first on a piece of paper, and sketch out any names and message before writing them straight onto the card. Paint a border to your own design with the black and yellow inks, then paint your hearts in red and blue poster paints, touching up the hearts with red ink. Metallic inks will brighten up any design, and in this case a light dusting of gold ink, applied with a large brush, has been used on the border of the card. Use a silver pen for small details and a special message.

MATERIALS
Papier mâché pulp (see pp. 9–10)
Old plastic container
2–3 dessertspoons of red drawing ink
Clingfilm
Petroleum jelly
1 A4 sheet of thin white card
Pencil
Various paintbrushes
Red and blue poster paints
Black Indian, yellow and red drawing inks; gold metallic drawing ink
Silver metallic pen
Thinned PVA medium (see p .9)

1

2

3

4

1 Take the papier mâché pulp and start to model the flower motifs for your greetings card. Roll a small ball of pulp in the palm of your hand, and press it flat onto a piece of clingfilm that has been smeared with petroleum jelly as a releasing agent. Form five or six petal shapes with the pulp, and carefully attach them to the centre of the flower. Leave the pulp flowers to dry and harden for about a week.

2 Fold the thin A4 card in half and start to put the flower shapes onto it. Move them into different positions until you think the design is just right, then trace around the flowers lightly with a pencil to mark their place on the card.

3 Remove the pulped flowers from the card and apply an undercoat of gesso to all of them. Leave to dry. Then decorate the flowers with the pearlized and poster paints. Finish with five coats of polyurethane varnish, leaving to dry between coats as detailed in the manufacturer's instructions.

4 With the inks and poster and pearlized paints, draw some simple leaves to form the background design on the card. Attach the papier mâché flowers to the card with some PVA medium at the points marked in pencil, pressing firmly into position. Finally, write your special message to suit the occasion on the inside of the card.

FLOWER GREETINGS CARD

Many occasions, such as birthdays, engagements and moving house, call for a greetings card, so this pretty, personalized card is bound to be well received. It is fun to make and does not take long.

Paint the flower motifs in light-gold, blue, mauve and white pearlized paints to produce delicate and shimmering colours. By adding yellow and orange

centres in poster paints the flowers become bright and fresh looking. The leaves are painted in a stylized design using different shades of blue, green and yellow poster paints and inks, plus some green pearlized paint to provide a little variation. The finished effect is simple, but striking.

Although papier mâché is a durable material, it is best to avoid sending this card by post, unless it is inside a padded package.

You can also adapt the greetings card for different occasions – you can make a teddy bear to celebrate a new baby, for example, or mould a horseshoe to say "good luck" to somebody.

MATERIALS
Papier mâché pulp (*see p. 9–10*)
Clingfilm
1 A4 sheet of thin white card
Pencil
Acrylic gesso
Various paintbrushes
Light-gold, blue, mauve, white and green pearlized acrylic paints
Yellow, orange, blue and green poster paints
Polyurethane varnish
Blue, green and yellow inks
Acrylic gesso
PVA medium

MATERIALS

Modelling clay
Petroleum jelly
Thinned PVA medium (see p. 9)
Flat-ended pasting brush
Short newspaper strips (see p. 9)
Craft knife
Acrylic gesso
Various paintbrushes
Blue, green and black drawing inks
Blue and green poster paints
White acrylic paint
Light-blue pearlized acrylic paint
Gloss polyurethane varnish
Small magnet
Strong metal glue

EASY LEVEL

WHALE FRIDGE MAGNET

This little blue whale makes a fun gift for children, or it can be used as a charming Christmas stocking filler. As a fridge magnet it will soon become a useful household item.

As you apply the layers of papier mâché to the whale mould, you will notice that you can model the key features, such as the tail, fins and domed head, with remarkable ease. It is also when you are applying layers around the facial area to form a hint of a nose, that you can give your whale a little bit of character. After all, a fridge magnet should be a bright and attractive object as a lot of important notes are pinned onto refrigerator doors in busy households nowadays.

The whale is painted in layers of bright-blue, green and black inks and poster paints. By adding a touch of light-blue pearlized and white acrylic paint, particularly to the side of the whale where the waves are lapping up, you help create a feeling of movement. By applying several coats of gloss polyurethane varnish to the magnet, you help to give the whale its suitably shiny, wet look.

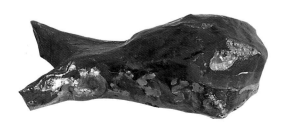

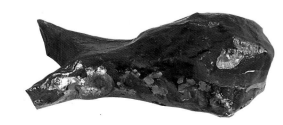

1

2

3

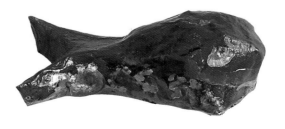

4

1 Soften some modelling clay and model a whale shape that is about 3½in (9cm) long, as shown. Keep the form very simple, just making a large, domed head and some tail fins.

2 Apply petroleum jelly all over the modelling-clay mould as a releasing agent. Then paste PVA medium onto the newspaper strips,

following the method for layering papier mâché onto a mould (see p. 12). Apply eight layers over the surface of the mould, leaving the underneath clear so that the modelling clay can easily be removed. Leave to dry for several hours between layers.

3 When the papier mâché has fully hardened, remove the modelling clay, digging it out

carefully with the help of a craft knife. Then apply a further eight layers of paper mâché strips over the base of the whale to cover the hole, and again leave to dry for several hours between layers.

4 Apply gesso as an undercoat to the whale, painting over the entire surface of the papier mâché with a small paintbrush. Use inks,

poster and acrylic paints to decorate the whale and to create the waves on the bottom edge. Finish the whale with five coats of gloss polyurethane varnish, leaving to dry between coats as detailed in the manufacturer's instructions. Finally, attach a small magnet to the base of the whale with some strong glue, and then place it in his rightful position on the refrigerator door.

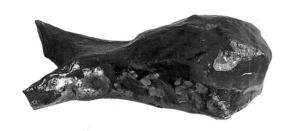

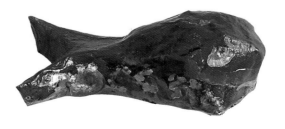

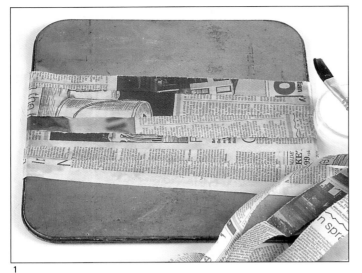

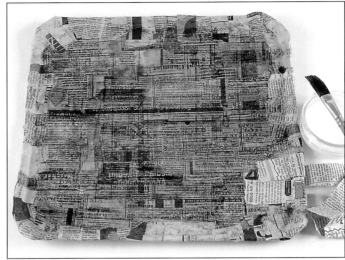

1

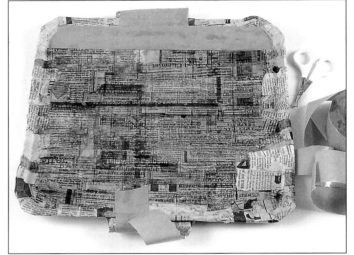

2

3

4

1 Smear the top surface and raised edges of the baking sheet with petroleum jelly to act as a releasing agent. Paste PVA medium onto the newspaper strips and apply them to the mould, following the method for layering papier mâché onto a mould (*see p. 12*). Build up the papier mâché to eight layers, working in alternate directions, and covering the raised edges on the mould. Leave to dry for several hours between layers.

2 Remove the papier mâché from the mould when it has fully hardened, and clean away any residue of petroleum jelly with

kitchen paper. Paste the shorter strips of newspaper and apply three layers around the tray's ridge to produce a firm, bold edge. Again, leave the papier mâché to dry for several hours between layers. When dry, trim as necessary with scissors.

3 To make the curved handles, measure and cut two pieces of thin cardboard 3½in (9cm) x 5½in (14cm) with the craft knife. Brush the corrugated side of the card with PVA medium and tightly roll it up until it is only 1in (2.5cm) wide. Secure in place with four pieces of gummed tape that extend from behind the

rolled card to the edge. When the handles have completely dried, apply five layers of shorter newspaper strips to cover over the rolled ends of the corrugated card.

4 Secure the handles onto the tray by first applying PVA medium to the flat edge of the handle and the edge of the curve. Place the handles opposite each other and tape to the back of the tray with the curved part of the handles fitting against the ridge. Use layers of tape to secure the handles in place, placing the tape over the top of the curve onto each side. Then put long strips of tape

horizontally onto both sides of the tray to hold both the taped handles in position. Next, apply an undercoat of gesso to all the surfaces. When dry, apply a blue base coat to the tray and the sides of the handles. Paste the strips of coloured tissue paper with some PVA medium and position them on the tray, horizontally and vertically, to form a plaid pattern. Accentuate the colours of the tissue paper with drawing inks, if preferred. Finally, to protect the tray's delicate surface, apply five coats of polyurethane varnish, leaving to dry between coats as detailed in the manufacturer's instructions .

EASY LEVEL

PLAID TRAY

Layers of coloured tissue paper have been used here to build up a stylish and fashionable plaid pattern on this tray. It has a bright, cheerful appeal and is perfect for serving appetizers at a cocktail party. It would also look equally good carrying sweets or jellies at a children's party.

Paint the base of the tray and the sides of the handles in deep blue poster paint or another colour in the design.

You then need to apply the pink, yellow, green and blue tissue strips (or your chosen colours) in several layers, fixing them to the tray with PVA medium in a criss-cross pattern.

When the tissue paper has dried, the colours can be enhanced by painting on corresponding colours in inks. An alternative is to cut out some shapes – flowers or leaves, for example – and paste them on top of the plaid pattern. You can then also apply this simple method of decoration to many other projects, such as plates dishes or bowls. The varnish will give the tray a glossy finish and protect it against spillages when it is being used.

MATERIALS
1 baking sheet for a mould
Petroleum jelly
2in (5cm) and short newspaper strips (*see p. 9*)
Thinned PVA medium (*see p. 9*)
Flat-ended pasting brush
Kitchen paper
Scissors, ruler, marker pen and craft knife
Cardboard and gummed tape
Various paintbrushes
Acrylic gesso
Blue poster paint; pink, yellow, green, white and blue inks
Coloured tissue paper, PVA medium, polyurethane varnish

1

3

4

1 Take each leaf and lay it face down on a piece of clingfilm. Apply some petroleum jelly as a releasing agent to the back of each leaf. Take some of the papier mâché pulp and press firmly onto the leaves so that each is covered with a thin layer. Leave the leaves to dry for about a week.

2 When the pulp has dried, remove it carefully from the leaves. There will be no residue of petroleum jelly with this method of applying pulp. Paint one side of the leaves with an undercoat of gesso, leave to dry, and then paint a further coat on the reverse side. Later, decorate the leaves with the coloured inks and poster paints. Finally, apply five coats of polyurethane varnish to each of the leaves, leaving them to dry between coats as detailed in the manufacturer's instructions .

3 To make a simple hanging structure you will need two pieces of triangular-ended balsa wood dowel. Each piece should measure about 1ft (30cm) long and ⅜in (1cm) wide. You will also need four finer square-ended rods: 2¾in (7cm) and 3⁄16in (4cm) wide. Using the tip of a craft knife, make a hole in both ends of each piece of wood and the rods. Insert a small pin eye into each hole and apply some wood glue to each.

4 Join the two longer dowels together to make a crosspiece as shown above. Apply some wood glue to the middle point of one piece of dowel and attach the other piece of dowel, flat side on, to make a cross shape. Use a craft knife to cut a little of the wood away on the middle point of the join so that you can insert a screw eye here. This fixing helps to reinforce the join and thread can be attached to it so that you can hang the mobile. Fix the four small rods to the four sections of the crosspiece by attaching two short pieces of thread from each rod's pin eye to the corresponding one on the crosspiece. Then hang a long thread from each pin eye on the rods. Paint the wood structure with the inks and paints in colours that complement the leaves. Then attach the leaves by piercing each leaf with a needle, feeding the thread through and tying a knot to secure. Add a small piece of modelling clay in a matching colour to the stem of each leaf to balance it, if necessary.

LEAF MOBILE

Real leaves have been used as the moulds in this project because they give a natural, delicate detail to the papier-mâché foliage. The leaves are so light that they will spin gently in the slightest breeze and conjure up an image of swirling autumn leaves.

Green, pink, yellow and blue drawing inks are ideal for decorating the leaves, as they collect in the veins and accentuate the natural detail. You can add in some lime-green, purple and brown poster paint for a more opaque finish.

Balance the leaves against each other when you hang them. Add a tiny amount of modelling clay in a matching colour to the stem of each leaf to act as a counterbalance, if needed. Deck the finished crosspiece with evergreens or dried foliage for a natural finish.

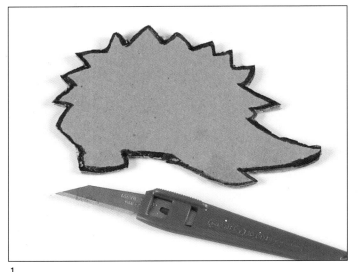

1

2

3

4

1 Draw in a hedgehog shape onto a piece of cardboard with the marker pen as shown. If you are unsure about drawing freehand onto the card, make a paper template and draw round the hedgehog, enlarging if necessary on the photocopier. Cut out the cardboard shape with a craft knife.

2 Apply the papier mâché pulp to the cardboard to a depth of about ⅜in (10mm). Use a small blob of pulp to form the eyes and nose. Then roll some small spike shapes and fix them onto the main part of the pulp in the appropriate places. Leave the papier mâché to dry for about a week.

3 When the papier mâché has dried, turn the model over. Paste PVA medium onto the newspaper strips and, following the method for layering papier mâché onto a mould (*see p. 12*), apply five layers to the mould. Leave each layer to dry for several hours before applying the next. Neaten ends with scissors.

4 Turn over, and add pulp for more spikes and to neaten. Dry for about a week, then apply some gesso. Next decorate with paints and later apply five coats of polyurethane varnish, drying between coats as detailed in the manufacturer's instructions. Finally, glue a magnet to the hedgehog's back.

MATERIALS

Cardboard

Marker pen

Paper template (optional)

Craft knife

Papier mâché pulp
(see pp. 9–10)

Flat-ended pasting brush

Thinned PVA medium (see p. 9)

Small pieces of newspaper
strips (see p. 9)

Scissors

Various paintbrushes

Acrylic gesso

Blue, red, black and green
poster paints

Pink and blue pearlized paints

Polyurethane varnish

Small magnet

Strong metal glue

INTERMEDIATE LEVEL

HEDGEHOG FRIDGE MAGNET

This brightly coloured hedgehog fridge magnet makes an original and light-hearted Christmas or birthday present, and will soon become a familiar friend on the refrigerator. Although it is only small in size, the hedgehog does require quite a lot of patience to make, as modelling the spikes on its back is quite tricky and can't be rushed. You might find it helpful to use a match-stick to make a smooth join at the base of each spike.

Decorate the hedgehog in black and green poster colours, using blue and red as a base coat. Paint the spikes red, and highlight them with some pink pearlized paint. Mark out the eyes with the green and black poster paints. Paint all over the hedgehog with the blue pearlized paint.

It is easy to adapt this method of modelling to make other appealing animals with spiky hair or fur. The models need not be designed as fridge magnets: you could try experimenting with three-dimensional models or animal figures in relief.

BUTTERFLY FRIDGE MAGNET

This giant butterfly painted in soft, pearlized colours makes a delightfully whimsical addition to any kitchen refrigerator. Although it is not that difficult to make, care needs to be taken when creating the wings. Check that the pulp on the wings has adhered properly to the main bulk of the body, and that the butterfly has been carefully reinforced underneath with the paper strips. As the wings dry they will rise slightly from the body, giving the butterfly a light and cheerful look. Paint the wings in a pearlized white paint and highlight them and the main body with dabs of mauve and blue. Add touches of the green paint on the body and decorate the head with light gold and a touch of pink.

This butterfly magnet can also be adapted into a mobile for a conservatory or garden room. Make several butterflies and instead of attaching a magnet to the base of each butterfly, fix a screw eye into the top of the body and hang from a simple wood frame (*see Leaf Mobile pp. 86–87*)

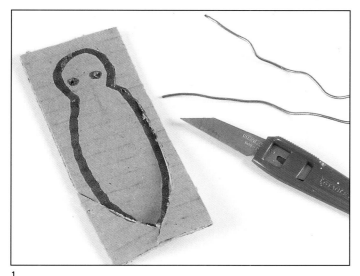

1

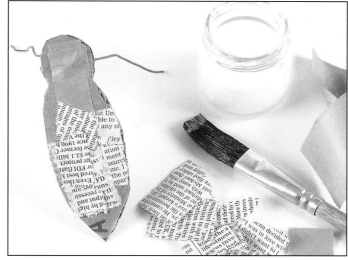

2

3

4

MATERIALS

| Cardboard and marker pen |
| Craft knife and scissors |
| Copper wire |
| Brown gummed tape |
| Thinned PVA medium (see p. 9) |
| Flat-ended pasting brush |
| Small newspaper strips (see p. 9) |
| Papier mâché pulp (see pp. 9–10) |
| Cling film and petroleum jelly |
| Various paintbrushes |
| Acrylic gesso |
| Mauve, blue, white, green, pink and light-gold pearlized acrylic paints |
| Polyurethane varnish |
| Magnet and strong metal glue |

1 Draw the outline of the butterfly's body onto a piece of cardboard as shown. The shape should be about 4in (10cm) in length. Mark the two spots on the head where the antennae will protrude, and pierce holes with the tip of a craft knife. Cut out the body shape with scissors and prepare a piece of copper wire about 4in (10cm) to be used bent in half for the antennae.

2 Thread the copper wire through the two holes, and secure to the base with two pieces of brown gummed tape. Paste PVA medium onto the small newspaper pieces and, following the method for layering papier mâché onto a mould (see p.12) apply five layers to the base. Allow the papier mâché to dry for several hours between layers, and then trim away any untidy newspaper ends with scissors.

3 Turn the butterfly right side up and roll small balls of papier mâché pulp to complete the antennae. Model a raised body and head from the pulp onto the cardboard, then attach more pulp to form the wings. Place the butterfly onto a piece of clingfilm that has been smeared with petroleum jelly as a releasing agent. Apply another layer of pulp over the body, head and wings and leave for about a week.

4 Apply two more layers of newspaper strips to the back of the butterfly to reinforce the wings. Dry for several hours between the layers, then apply a coat of gesso to the butterfly. Decorate with pearlized paints. Later, finish with five coats of polyurethane varnish, leaving to dry between coats as detailed in the manufacturer's instructions. Finally, attach a magnet to the reverse side of the butterfly using strong glue.

INTERMEDIATE LEVEL

LETTER RACK

A letter rack is always useful to have in your home as a place to keep letters and bills tidy and easy to find. Making a special one to give as a gift to a friend or a relative will make it a particularly treasured item.

A collage of postage stamps decorates the letter rack, which is then veiled with a thin wash of inks and paint to give an aged look and a slight hint of past foreign adventures.

Use PVA medium to apply old postage stamps (packets of these can be bought cheaply from newsagents) over the outside of the box. Overlap and layer the stamps for a special collage effect, then rub the surface with a little white acrylic paint. Follow this with some pink and yellow ink to achieve a subtle, misty effect. Contrast this subdued style with a bold black and white pattern around the base and along the edges of opening of the letter rack.

The inside is finished with a dark metallic look, which is made by mixing black Indian ink with green and blue pearlized paints, while the base is covered in some red poster paint.

MATERIALS

Cardboard box and cardboard for base, ruler, marker pen

Craft knife, PVA medium and brown gummed tape

Thinned PVA medium (*see p. 9*)

Flat-ended pasting brush

1in (2.5cm) newspaper strips (*see p. 9*)

Acrylic gesso

Various paintbrushes

Packets of used postage stamps

White acrylic paint

Pink, yellow and black Indian drawing ink

Green and blue pearlized paints

Red poster paint

Polyurethane varnish

1

2

3

4

1 Take a 8in x 10in x 3½in (20cm x 25cm x 9cm) box. If you can't find a box, then you can make one out of cardboard. Next, measure halfway up the box and draw a line with a ruler horizontally across the front. Then draw two diagonal lines down both sides of the box from the back, top corners to the line at the front of the box, as shown. Cut a 5in x 10in (13cm x 25cm) cardboard base

2 Use a craft knife to cut away the marked section on the box. Apply PVA medium to the underside of the box and place on the base in the centre. Secure with gummed brown paper. Tape over any staples.

3 Paste PVA medium onto the newspaper strips and, following the method for layering papier mâché onto a mould (*see p. 12*), apply five layers over the box and base. Dry for several hours between layers.

4 When dry, trim the papier mâché, and apply a coat of gesso over the letter rack. Then decorate with the stamps, inks and paints. To finish, apply five coats of polyurethane varnish, leaving to dry between coats as detailed in the manufacturer's instructions.

1

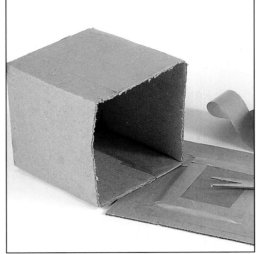

3

5

2

4

6

1 Take the cardboard carton or make one to the same dimensions. You will then need to cut a piece of flat cardboard about 7in (17.5cm) square to use as a lid, and two cardboard squares with sides measuring 4in (10cm) to make an insert for the lid.

2 Using brown gummed tape, secure the cardboard inserts together in the centre of the lid and cover any staples with tape.

3 Paste PVA medium onto the newspaper strips and, following the method for layering papier mâché onto a mould (*see p. 12*), apply five layers to the box. Leave to dry for several hours between layers.

4 The next stage is to make the shell reliefs for the lid. Use modelling clay to make relief moulds from three halves of bivalve shells. Soften a piece of modelling clay and flatten it in your hand. Press the shell firmly into the clay and remove to reveal the details of the shell. Curve the modelling clay edges upward in your hand and place it on clingfilm, smeared with petroleum jelly.

5 Carefully apply petroleum jelly inside the moulds to act as a releasing agent. Take some papier mâché pulp and press it into each mould. Leave to dry for about a week.

6 When the pulp has hardened, release from the moulds and remove any residue of petroleum jelly with kitchen paper and a little lighter fuel, if necessary. Brush PVA medium onto the base of the shell reliefs and arrange on the lid in a simple design. When they have fully bonded, apply a coat of gesso to the box and lid. Decorate with the paints and inks. Finally, finish with five coats of polyurethane varnish, leaving to dry between coats as detailed in the manufacturer's instructions.

MATERIALS

5in (13cm) square cardboard box and cardboard
Ruler, marker pen, scissors and brown gummed tape
Thinned PVA medium (*see p. 9*)
Flat-ended pasting brush
1in (2.5in) newspaper strips (*see p. 9*)
Modelling clay and bivalve shells
Cling film and petroleum jelly
Kitchen paper
Lighter fuel (optional)
PVA medium, acrylic gesso
Various paintbrushes
Blue, green and light-gold pearlized paints
Blue, pink and yellow drawing inks
White acrylic paint
Polyurethane varnish

SEASHELL STORAGE BOX

Everyone wants a box to show off the different seashells that they have collected from their various holidays. This one is perfect to display with shells and it also makes a very attractive gift. It can be filled with small bottles of perfumed shampoo, bath oil beads and shell-shaped soaps to make it even more appealing.

The whole of the box and its lid have been decorated with shimmering blue and green and a touch of light- gold pearlized paints, which help to give the shell shapes a delicate feel and a note of realism. If you want to deepen the effect of the marine colours, dapple some blue ink over the first layer of paint, and then highlight with touches of white acrylic paint. To give the box a weathered or slightly distressed appearance, trickle some drawing ink over the wet pearlized paint and then dab gently with a piece of kitchen paper.

To create the interesting spiral shell design on the front face of the box, use some white acrylic paint. Soften the strength of the background colours a little by applying tiny amounts of blue, pink and yellow inks before the paint is thoroughly dry.

By varnishing the finished project you will protect the papier mâché from damage and also help to enhance the look of the shimmering and dappled paintwork effects.

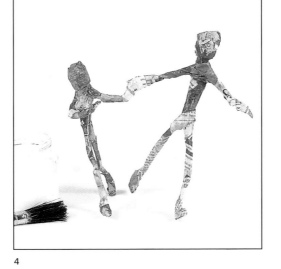

1

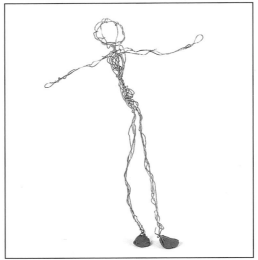

2

3

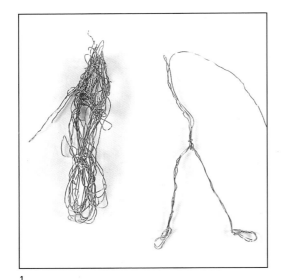

4

MATERIALS

Fine copper wire
Wire cutters
Modelling clay
Thinned PVA medium (*see p. 9*)
Flat-ended pasting brush
Small newspaper strips (*see p. 9*)
Acrylic gesso
Various paintbrushes
White pearlized acrylic paint
Black poster paint
Black Indian drawing ink
Polyurethane varnish

1 Using the copper wire, start to form the first dancing figure by making the figure's body and limbs, twisting several widths of the wire back on and around itself.

2 Continue to form the body and add a three-dimensional head onto the shoulders. When you are satisfied with the result, stand the figure up by attaching a small amount of modelling clay to each foot. Repeat the process to make the second, slightly smaller figure.

3 Paste PVA medium onto the newspaper strips, following the method for layering papier mâché onto a mould (*see p. 12*), and apply to the wire moulds. Build up the papier mâché strips to a depth of five layers, covering the modelling clay feet as you do this. Leave to dry for about four days.

4 Use some more pasted newspaper strips to join the dancing figures firmly together, so that they appear to be holding hands. Leave to dry for about a day, or until hard, and then apply a coat of gesso to the papier mâché figures. Later, decorate them with the pearlized and poster paints and inks. Finally, apply five coats of polyurethane varnish to protect them, leaving to dry between coats as detailed in the manufacturer's instructions.

INTERMEDIATE LEVEL

DANCING FIGURES

These simple figures made from a wire mould are very easy to make. They can look equally attractive placed on a glass display shelf or on a side table that is subtly lighted.

To make the figures, however, a little bit of patience is needed to find exactly the right point at which both figures will stand up. Once you have found this, and joined them together at the hands, they will remain very stable. Aim to keep the theme simple by painting the figures in one uniform colour. Try decorating the pair with a single layer of pearlized white paint, or another colour of your choice, over the gesso undercoat. A mere suggestion of facial features is given by applying a little black poster paint and black Indian ink with a fine brush.

You could also adapt this technique of model making to create much larger figures and animals. But instead of pliable wire, you will need to using some chicken wire to build up the main structure around which to form the layers of papier mâché.

1 The snake in this project is made up from six sections, each decreasing a little in size. Draw the sections for the snake onto the cardboard with a marker pen. The head section is 2¼in (6cm) and the final tail piece is 1in (2.5cm). Your measurements need not be exact, but use these for guidance. Cut out the sections using a craft knife.

2 Mould some papier mâché pulp onto the top surface of each section to a depth of up to 1in (2.5cm). Create a forked tongue and features on the snake's face, and extend the final tail piece into a point. Leave all the pieces to dry for about a week.

3 When the papier mâché has dried, turn each section over. Then paste PVA medium onto the newspaper strips and apply five layers to each base, following the method for layering papier mâché onto a mould (see p. 12).

4 To make large eyes for the snake, model a pulp bead onto a cotton-bud stem with one end removed, first smearing with petroleum jelly as a releasing agent. After about a week, slice the hard bead in half and attach each piece to the snake's face with PVA medium.

5 Lay out the sections of the snake to see how it will fit together, then apply a coat of gesso to all sections. When dry, decorate with the bright poster colours. To finish apply five coats of polyurethane varnish, leaving to dry between coats as detailed in the manufacturer's instructions. Finally, assemble the snake by attaching screw eyes to the sections and linking them together with a couple of jump rings. Attach a magnet with glue to the base of each section and hold firmly to secure. Then place the snake on the refrigerator.

1

2

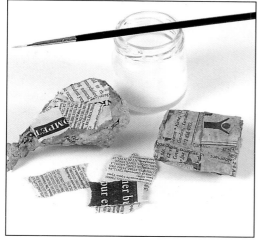

3

ADVANCED LEVEL

SNAKE FRIDGE MAGNET

This bright snake with its vivid jungle colours won't be missed by anyone as it slithers across the front of the refrigerator! Paint each poster colour separately onto the gesso undercoat. The "V" snake pattern painted in red, bright blue, lime green and purple has a bold, dynamic effect. Paint the eyes in yellow to stand out and add some black to the tongue. You may of course prefer to paint bright spots or scales on this vibrant snake.

4

MATERIALS

Cardboard

Marker pen

Craft knife

Papier mâché pulp
(see pp. 9–10)

Thinned PVA medium (see p. 9)

Flat-ended pasting brush

Short newspaper strips,
(see p. 9)

Cotton buds and petroleum jelly

Acrylic gesso

Various paintbrushes

Red, purple, lime-green,
yellow, bright-blue and black
poster paints

Polyurethane varnish

Screw eyes and jump rings

Small magnets

Strong metal glue

5

1

2

3

4

5

6

1 To make this display shelf you will need a cardboard carton about 12in (30cm) square and with a depth of 4in (10cm). If you cannot find anything similar, then it is quite easy to make a box to the same dimensions from cardboard. In addition to the box itself, you will need to mark out a piece of cardboard 8in x 12in (20cm x 30cm), and fold it in half, to use as the centre shelf.

2 Use strips of brown gummed tape to secure the shelf in position across the centre of the box. Then tape over any exposed staples, if necessary.

3 Apply the pulp, following the method for pulping papier mâché onto a mould (see p. 13), over the entire surface of the cardboard structure to a thickness of about ¼in (6mm). You may have to do this in several layers to allow the pulp to adhere properly. Leave to dry for about a week.

4 Choose some middle-sized leaves that will fit onto the box. Lay the leaves face down onto a sheet of clingfilm and apply petroleum jelly as a releasing agent to the back of the leaves. Apply a thin layer of pulp to the leaves.

5 Prop one of the leaves up against a block, or piece of card, to produce a right-angle shape to hang over the edge of the shelf. Set aside to dry for about a week.

6 Release the pulp from the leaves and fix the moulded shapes to the display shelf with PVA medium. Then apply a coat of gesso over the entire project. Later, decorate the shelf with the poster paints and inks. Finish the project with five coats of polyurethane varnish, leaving to dry between coats as detailed in the manufacturer's instructions.

DISPLAY SHELF

This attractive and original display shelf is decorated with ochre, orange and brown leaves to give it a warm, autumnal look. You can use it in the kitchen to display some vegetables or elsewhere to show a mixture of objects, such as pine cones, conkers, fossils and stones, found out on walks.

The rugged texture of the shelf makes a perfect surface to paint a mottling of yellow, brown, green, orange and red colours in poster paints. Highlight the red and yellow with some drawing inks to create more variance in the finished colour. You should aim to create a dappled and variegated effect. The leaves can be decorated in exactly the same way, or alternatively they can be given a more detailed treatment using a fine paintbrush to apply the colours.

The finished shelf can just be free-standing on a surface, or it is possible to mount it onto a wall by attaching a small bracket to the back. Use small screws to go through the papier mâché frame. If any hairline cracks should start to appear on the surface, apply some wood filler to cover them up.

MATERIALS
Cardboard carton
1 piece of cardboard
Marker pen, scissors and ruler
Brown gummed tape
2 amounts of papier mâché pulp (see pp. 9–10)
Leaves suitable as moulds
Clingfilm
Petroleum jelly
Various paintbrushes
PVA medium
Acrylic gesso
Yellow, brown, green, orange and red poster paints
Red and yellow drawing inks
Polyurethane varnish

1 This mirror frame is based on three pieces of cardboard. Each piece, A, B and C, is the same size: 5in (12.5cm) wide, and 7in (17. 5cm) high. Measure a vertical line 1in (2.5cm) down from the middle of the top of each piece. Then using a ruler, draw a horizontal line across the front of each piece at this point. Draw slanting lines from the middle, top point to meet up with the horizontal line to make a triangular shape. Cut along these lines with a craft knife.

2 Place a small rectangular mirror in the centre of pieces B and C and draw around its outline on each card. On piece C, measure ¼in (6mm) inside the line and draw a rectangle within the mirror outline. Cut out the rectangle on B, and the inner rectangle on C (as shown). The mirror will sit behind B, with C placed over B as a frame.

3 Apply ¼in (6mm) papier mâché pulp to the backing piece A, and to the front piece C. Press small shells into the pulp on C, and leave to dry for about a week.

4 Use a strong glue to stick the mirror in a central position on the cardboard side of A. Press B in place over the mirror and secure with PVA medium.

5 When the pulp is completely dry, place C on top of B and glue firmly in place.

6 Cover the mirror's edges with a layer of pulp and leave to dry for about a week. Apply gesso to the papier mâché, leave to dry, then decorate with the pearlized paints and ink. Finish with five coats of polyurethane varnish, leaving to dry between coats as detailed in the manufacturer's instructions. Fix a mirror hook on the back, if you intend to hang the finished project.

SHELL MIRROR

Decorated with real shells, and painted with subtle, pastel paint colours, this mirror makes a delightful birthday gift for a friend or an attractive addition to your own dressing table at home. Alternatively, you can fix a mirror hook to the back and hang it up in a bathroom that has been decorated with a seaside colour scheme.

If you don't have your own collection of shells that you can use to decorate the mirror, you can just buy a bag of small shells from a craft shop.

At first sight this mirror may look complicated to make. However, if you take your time and follow all the steps carefully, it is not difficult and will give a very satisfying and professional-looking result.

You may like to decorate the inner edge of the top frame before you secure it in place and pulp around the outer edges. However, if you choose not to do this, apply the gesso undercoat and the paints with a small paintbrush. Then wipe away any excess paint from the mirror with some kitchen paper before it starts to dry.

Decorate the mirror surround in white, pink, light-gold and green pearlized paint colours to echo the iridescent appearance of the shells. You can then add a dusting of gold ink with a paintbrush to give the frame's surface that extra richness and sparkle.

If any of the shells become loose after a while, they can easily be refixed to the mirror with some strong glue.

1

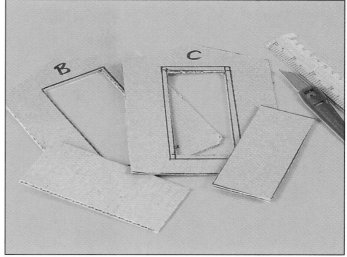

2

MATERIALS
Cardboard

Ruler and marker pen

Rectangular mirror

Small craft knife

Papier mâché pulp
(*see pp. 9–10*)

A bag of small shells

Strong glue

PVA medium

Various paintbrushes

Acrylic gesso

White, pink, light-gold and
green pearlized paints

Gold drawing ink

Polyurethane varnish

Mirror hook

3

4

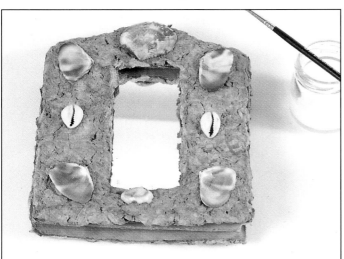

5

6

MONKEY BOOK ENDS

These cheerful, cheeky monkey book ends might be just what it takes to encourage younger bookworms to do the unthinkable – tidy their bedrooms.

Model your monkeys carefully, looking at photographs for reference if necessary. Remember that the monkey is reversed on the second book end, so the two face one another when in use.

The monkeys are painted in brown and light-gold poster and pearlized paints with their features highlighted with red poster paint and black ink. They are shown against a simple jungle scene and are seated among brightly coloured plants and flowers. Paint the sky with blue ink and the sun in yellow and orange poster paints. Use the green, turquoise, red and purple paints and blue and green inks to create the vibrant jungle scene. You might also prefer to add more monkeys or other exotic animals into the scene.

MATERIALS
Cardboard and ruler
Scissors and craft knife
2 matchboxes
Modelling clay, glue
Brown gummed tape
Flat-ended pasting brush
Thinned PVA medium (see p. 9)
1in (2.5cm) newspaper strips (see p. 9)
Papier mâché pulp (see pp. 9–10)
Various paintbrushes
Acrylic gesso
Brown, red, yellow, orange, green, turquoise, and purple poster paints
Light-gold pearlized acrylic paint
Blue, black Indian and green drawing inks
Polyurethane varnish

1 The monkey book ends are based on two pieces of rectangular cardboard measuring 21cm x 12cm (8¼ x 4 ¾in). Measure 3¾in (9cm) along the length of the card and score a line vertically down the card using a ruler and a craft knife. The step on which each monkey is seated is formed around a matchbox. Put a little modelling clay inside each empty matchbox to act as a weight.

2 Fold the cards along the scored edge and glue the matchboxes in a central position on the shorter portion of the card. Reinforce in position with several pieces of brown gummed tape.

3 Paste PVA medium onto the newspaper strips and, following the method for layering papier mâché onto a mould (*see p. 12*), build up five layers to cover each structure. Set aside to dry for several hours between layers.

4 Take the papier mâché pulp and begin to form the figure of a seated monkey in profile on the step. Start by modelling the body and limbs, and then take a small ball of pulp and start to form the shape of the head.

5 Continue to model the monkey by adding details to the facial features, and modelling a long tail over the edge of the step. Then make the second monkey on the other book end so that it faces in the opposite direction. Leave the papier mâché to dry thoroughly for about a week.

6 When the pulp has dried, apply a coat of gesso to each model. Later, decorate with inks, poster and pearlized paints. Finish with five coats of polyurethane varnish, leaving to dry between coats as detailed in the manufacturer's instructions.

1

2

3

4

5

6

ADVANCED LEVEL

STRAW PICTURE FRAME

The final project in this book combines both methods of papier mâché plus some freehand modelling. It is quite a challenging project to do and requires a little extra patience to achieve the right finish. The result is a very individual and softly coloured picture frame. Lightly painted and decorated with some real straw or dried grass fibres embedded in the pulp, it has an earthy, very natural appeal.

Decide on the photograph you intend to frame before starting to decorate. A light-gold pearlized paint makes a good base colour, then add in some white acrylic paint and pink and yellow inks, or other colours that echo those that predominate in the photograph or picture you are framing.

1

2

MATERIALS

Modelling clay
Petroleum jelly
Clingfilm
Straw and dried grass (available from pet shops)
Papier mâché pulp (see pp. 9–10)
Ruler
Small piece of Perspex
Craft knife
Protective eye mask
Flat-ended pasting brush
Thinned PVA medium (see p. 9)
1in (2.5cm) newspaper strips (see p. 9)
Various paintbrushes
Acrylic gesso
Light-gold pearlized acrylic paint
White acrylic paint
Pink and yellow inks
Polyurethane varnish
Brown gummed tape

3

4

1 The mould for this project is made using some lengths of modelling clay that are three ribs or 1¼in (3cm) wide. Cut two pieces 4¾in (12cm) long, and another two pieces 3⅛in (8cm) long. Apply some petroleum jelly as a releasing agent to a sheet of clingfilm. Build a rectangular frame onto the clingfilm with the modelling clay and then apply some more petroleum jelly to the inside area.

2 Lay some strands of the straw or dried grass on the clingfilm, placing them along the inside edge of the modelling clay.

3 Take some papier mâché pulp and cover the straw fibres to a depth of ⅜in (1cm). Work outward from the mould towards the frame's centre until the pulp is 1in (2.5cm) wide.

4 Add another layer of pulp that is half the width of the first layer and fill up to the top of the modelling-clay mould, as shown. Leave the pulp to dry – it may take several weeks to harden fully at room temperature as it is such a thick layer.

5 When the pulp is completely dry, remove the modelling-clay mould. Use a ruler to check the

dimensions of the empty oblong area in the centre, and cut a piece of Perspex to a size that will fit neatly behind the inner oblong. To cut the Perspex, first score the shape carefully with a craft knife and then simply snap the Perspex along the line (it is important to wear a protective eye mask while you are doing this).

6 Cut a piece of cardboard to fit over the back of the picture frame, but within the limits of the outer ridge of papier mâché. Paste PVA medium onto all the newspaper strips and, following the method for

5

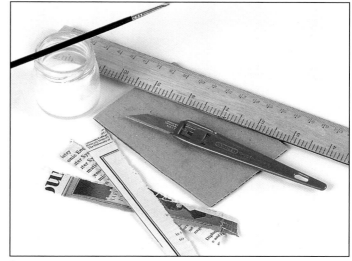

6

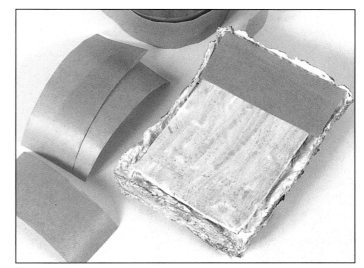

7

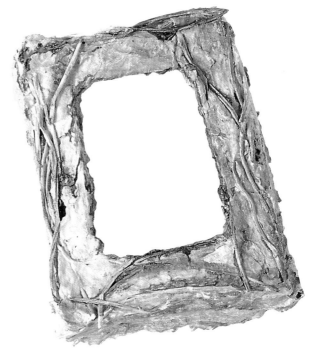

8

layering papier mâché onto a mould (*see p. 12*), build up five layers over the back and card edges. Dry for several hours between each layer.

7 Apply a coat of gesso to the frame. Leave to dry and then decorate with the pearlized and acrylic paints and inks. To protect the frame, finish with five coats of polyurethane varnish, leaving to dry between coats as detailed in the manufacturer's instructions.

8 Place the Perspex in the frame and fit your chosen photograph or illustration behind it. Fit the

backing card over the frame and then tape it firmly in place using some strips of brown gummed tape. Apply an undercoat of gesso all over the back. Later when dry, paint in the same pearlized and acrylic paints and inks to match the colour scheme of the rest of the frame.

INDEX

ACKNOWLEDGMENTS

THE PUBLISHERS AND AUTHOR WOULD LIKE TO THANK THE
FOLLOWING PEOPLE AND ORGANIZATIONS FOR THEIR GENEROUS HELP AND SUPPORT IN THE
PRODUCTION OF THIS BOOK:

SPECIAL THANKS TO

JIM MANSON FOR HIS ASSISTANCE WITH THE WRITING

JILL HLALO FOR TECHNICAL ADVICE

CHRIS MORLEY FOR CHECKING PROOFS

KATHIE GILL FOR INDEXING

USEFUL ADDRESSES

W H SMITH & SON LTD. – BRANCHES THROUGHOUT THE UK
(*Suppliers of paints, inks and other materials*)

THE BEAD SHOP, 43 NEAL STREET, COVENT GARDEN,
LONDON WC2H 9PJ
(*Beads and findings by mail order*)

L CORNELISSEN & SON LTD., FINE ARTISTS' MATERIALS,
105 GREAT RUSSELL STREET, LONDON WC1B 3RY
(*Paints by mail order*)

BIBLIOGRAPHY

TOLTER, JANE, *THE REGENCY & VICTORIAN CRAFTS,*
WARD LOCK LTD, 1969